Basic
PICTURE FRAMING

All the Skills and Tools You Need to Get Started

Amy Cooper, editor

Debbie Smith-Voight, CPF
framing consultant

Photographs by
Alan Wycheck

STACKPOLE
BOOKS

0 11557 03178 2

Published by
STACKPOLE BOOKS
5067 Ritter Road
Mechanicsburg, PA 17055
www.stackpolebooks.com

Printed in China

10 9 8 7 6 5 4 3 2

First edition

Cover design by Tracy Patterson

Cover painting: Swing Time Two *by Jeff Surrett, courtesy of Deljou Art Group*

Library of Congress Cataloging-in-Publication Data

Basic picture framing : all the skills and tools you need to get started / Amy Cooper, editor ; Debbie Smith-Voight, framing consultant ; photographs by Alan Wycheck.
   p. cm.
   ISBN-13: 978-0-8117-3178-2
   ISBN-10: 0-8117-3178-2
 1. Picture frames and framing—Technique. I. Cooper, Amy.
II. Smith-Voight, Debbie.

N8550.B357   2005
749'.7—dc22

2005015140

Contents

Acknowledgments

This book came about through the cooperative effort of a number of talented people.

First and foremost, I'd like to thank Debbie Smith-Voight, owner of Smith Custom Framing in New Cumberland, Pennsylvania, for contributing her expertise, time, and enthusiasm to the project. Without her, it wouldn't have been possible. She demonstrated the techniques, provided space and equipment for the photo shoots, and showed me the endless possibilities for color and texture in mats and frames. And you just have to like a woman who brings her dog to work with her. Thanks also to Yvonne Wilson at Smith Custom Framing, who knew where things were when Debbie wasn't there and helped greatly with the photo shoots.

Alan Wycheck, a cool guy to work and talk politics with, lent his great photography skills and his talented eye to the process. His vision in the previous books in this series helped shape this project.

Mark Allison, Chris Chappell, Caroline Stover, and Tracy Patterson at Stackpole Books gave the book its lovely design and contributed ideas that were greatly appreciated. They also made sure it all made sense. Thanks for your patience, all.

Amy Wagner cast her expert eye over the pages and did her usual outstanding job. Thanks, Amy!

Kyle Weaver, also at Stackpole, took on more than his share of our workload so I could in turn take on this project, and for that, and the sushi, I am grateful.

—Amy Cooper

Introduction

Picture framing consists of a set of simple skills—measuring, cutting mats, choosing and constructing frames, and putting all of the elements together. With practice, these skills are easy to learn, and they don't require a lot of expensive equipment or a large workshop. For less than $100, you can mat and frame pictures at your kitchen table, if you like.

But picture framing is also an art. The play of color and texture between mat, frame, and subject make the entire finished piece a work of art in its own right, and the possibilities are nearly endless for the different looks you can create with simple changes in mat or frame.

It is the aim of this book to teach the basics of both the art and the craft of picture framing. It will give you a basic equipment list and outline the skills you will need to mat and frame photographs, paintings, and even needlework. It will teach you how to build kit frames and construct simple wooden picture frames. It will also cover framing stretched canvases and larger pieces, including how to safely hang them for display. Hopefully, this book will also lead you to experiment as you explore the artistic side of matting and framing, trying out new colors in your mats and different materials in your frames. You are encouraged to look for framed art whenever possible, to study these elements, and to determine what your own tastes are and how to bring them back to the worktable.

1

Materials

Most of the tools and equipment you will need to mat, mount, and frame for yourself can be purchased at your local craft shop or art supply store. Check your local phone directory for stores near you (also see Resources on page 101).

Matting

HANDHELD MAT CUTTER AND SPARE BLADES

Available at most art supply shops, handheld mat cutters come in a variety of shapes and sizes. The model shown here, the Alto's model 45, is designed to be used with a more complicated mat cutting system but works fine on its own. It costs around $35, but you can spend as little as $20 to get a service-able handheld cutter. Better-quality cutters will have lines alongside the blade that make it easier to know where to start and end your cut. Spare blades come separately, usually in packs of five or six for around $2. Since having a sharp blade in your mat cutter is very important, be sure to purchase at least one pack.

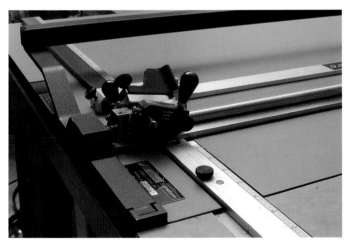

TABLETOP MAT CUTTER

Tabletop cutters allow for quicker, easier work when cutting mats, because the marking and measuring are simplified. Tabletop cutters are more expensive than handheld cutters, however, and many of those in the lower price ranges are fairly small and will not allow you to do larger projects. If you will be cutting smaller mats on a frequent basis, they are well worth the invest-ment. Expect to pay $75 to $150 for a tabletop mat cutter of reasonable quality. You will also need spare blades.

T-SQUARE AND STRAIGHT EDGE

Metal straight edges are best. Plastic, plain wood, and metal-edged wooden rulers are okay for measuring, but they may be dinged, nicked, or cut by the blade of the cutter and result in a crooked cut. Choose one with a non-slip backing such as cork to prevent sliding.

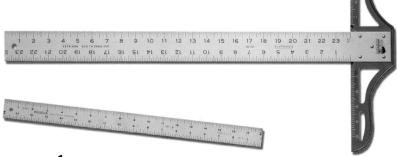

Your Workspace

You don't need a great deal of room to do your own matting and framing, nor do you need a specialized workshop area. A wide tabletop, big enough to allow your work to lay flat, is sufficient. For larger pieces of matboard, you can even use the floor. Remember to protect surfaces from the sharp edges of the cutting tools by doing your cutting on a cutting board or a thick piece of cardboard.

TAPE MEASURE
It is handy to have a tape measure on hand for spot-checking measurements when you don't want to lift your T-square or straight edge out of place.

UTILITY KNIFE AND SPARE BLADES
Either a standard box-cutter utility knife or one with snap-off disposable blades is suitable. Both can be purchased at craft stores, hardware stores, and art supply shops, along with extra blades.

PENCIL
A sharp pencil is needed for marking lines on the matboard. Have some scrap mat or paper handy for figuring measurements as well.

SINGLE-EDGE RAZOR BLADES
Useful for finishing undercut mat corners. Razor blades should be handled with great care, and double-edge blades should be avoided, because there is no dull edge to grasp with your fingers.

EMERY BOARD
Can be used to lightly sand the rough edge of a mat if your blade is dull and you get a ragged cut. Can also be used to fix small tears hanging from the corners if the matboard does not fall away cleanly.

SOFT ERASER
Can be used to burnish the inside bevel of the cut mat; also used to remove small smudges of dirt from the face of the mat or visible pencil lines from any part of the work.

MATBOARD

Available from art supply stores and some framing shops in a variety of colors, matboard comes in standard-size sheets of 32 x 40 inches and 40 x 60 inches. The two major manufacturers of most matboard are Crescent and Bainbridge.

There are a few different types of matboard generally available that are suitable for framing purposes. *Decorative matboard*, also called non-conservation matboard, is wood pulp that has been buffered by a chemical process to seal the acids into the interior of the board. The buffering process isn't permanent, and with time the center core can yellow. There is also a potential for acid burn on the artwork if it comes into contact with the mat, and the mat or the artwork may eventually fade and turn brown. Decorative matboard is relatively inexpensive, costing around $8 for a standard 32 x 40 sheet at a framing supply store. If you are simply framing decorative pieces that are not intended to last more than about three years and that are not particularly valuable, decorative matboard is suitable, but it is recommended that you spend a few extra dollars and buy at least a conservation-quality matboard.

Conservation-quality matboard is any kind that is acid-free. It won't stain or burn the artwork over time. There are a couple different grades of conservation matboard. *Alpha cellulose matboard* is a wood-pulp board that is pH-neutralized. A standard sheet will cost around $10 to $12. *Cotton rag matboard* is made of 100 percent cotton fibers rather than manmade or wood-pulp materials. It is unbuffered and undyed and naturally acid-free, and it will not burn the work or fade with time. For this reason, it is used in the framing of museum pieces and valuable or rare historic documents. It is the most expensive type of conservation matboard, with a standard sheet costing somewhere around $16. For the purposes of a home framing project, regular conservation-quality materials serve just as well.

4

FOAM BOARD

Foam board is a piece of polystyrene sandwiched between sheets of paper. Generally, it is used for mounting artwork, although it can be used for matting and several varieties of colored foam board are available for this use. When cut with a beveled edge, the contrasting inner color adds a nice touch to the framed work. It comes in standard thicknesses of $^1/_8$, $^3/_{16}$, $^1/_4$, and $^3/_8$ inches ($^3/_{16}$-inch is the most widely used). Acid-free foam board is readily available and is what you should use with all your projects. Foam board is not suitable for any framing or mounting technique which will expose it to temperatures in excess of 105 degrees F. Very light and rigid, it is ideal as mounting material for most projects, can be used as backing as well, and is easy to cut. It can be purchased in large sheets, similar to uncut matboard, at art supply and picture-framing supply stores for around $5 a sheet.

ACID-FREE DOUBLE-SIDED TAPE

Used to hold matboards to backing material and in making multiple mats, acid-free double-sided tape is available in refillable rollers for around $8, or you can buy a disposable version for about $4 at art and photo supply stores. Be sure the packaging specifies it as "acid-free." Acidic adhesives can damage and discolor matboard and can burn the artwork being framed. Larger professional-grade dispensers are also available for around $40, but the smaller versions work quite well for most home mounting and framing projects.

FILMOPLAST AND BURNISHER

Filmoplast is an acid-free adhesive that works well for mounting and is available for around $8 at art supply shops. You will need some type of burnishing tool to use with it, since it needs to be thoroughly smoothed once in place. Even the back of a soup spoon will work.

PHOTO CORNERS

Readily available in a variety of sizes at most craft stores and art supply shops, adhesive-backed photo corners work well for mounting artwork to backing material. Be sure the corners are acid-free. (Most are, because acid damages photographs as well.) A pack will cost around $3 or $4.

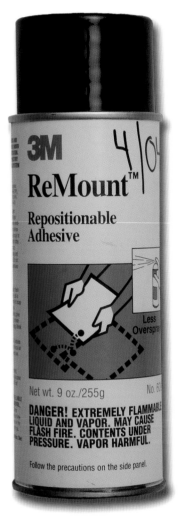

SPRAY ADHESIVE

Spray adhesives are not reversible (the artwork cannot later be separated from the mount without harm); they are used for mounting things such as posters—larger works of limited value—and some photographs. They can be purchased at art supply and craft shops for around $7.

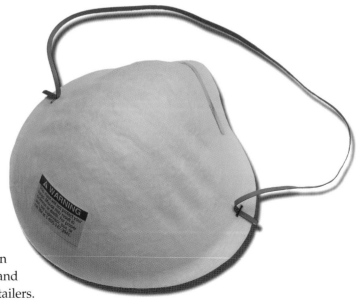

SAFETY MASK

Because of the toxic nature of the fumes, it is recommended that you wear a safety mask (and work in a well-ventilated area or outdoors) when using spray adhesives. These can be found at most hardware stores and home-improvement retailers.

Mounting Needlework

Mounting needlework is a specialized process that requires a few additional tools.

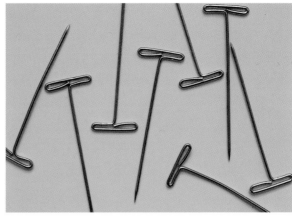

UPHOLSTERY THREAD AND NEEDLE

Regular thread is not strong enough to hold the backing of a needlework mount together. The needle you use should be large enough to work with easily.

STRAIGHT PINS

Large pins are used to anchor the corners of the mounted piece while the back is sewn.

Smaller straight pins are used to align the needlework along the sides to keep it straight while sewing.

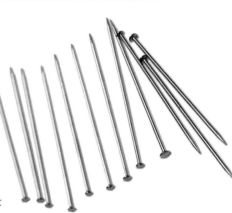

CRAFT SCISSORS

You will need scissors to cut the upholstery thread.

RUBBER GLOVES

These keep your needlework clean by protecting it from the oils on your hands. They also provide a little extra traction for your fingertips when you are aligning the cloth along the edges of the backing material.

7

Framing

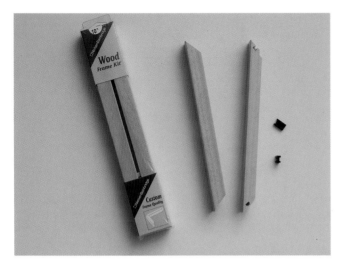

WOODEN FRAME KIT

Wooden frames are available in easy-to-assemble kits at most art supply shops. A typical kit includes small contoured brads to hold the corners together. Sides of equal length are sold in pairs, allowing you to choose the size of your frame by purchasing the lengths you need. For example, for an 8 x 10 frame, you simply buy one pair of 8-inch pieces and one pair of 10-inch pieces. The price depends on the size, but for an 8 x 10-inch frame, the cost should be around $20 total.

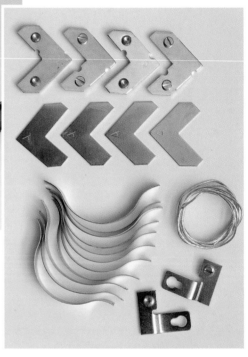

METAL FRAME KIT

Metal frame kits are also available at most art supply stores. Like the wooden frame kits, they come in paired packages, so to make an 8 x 10-inch frame, you'd buy one kit with 8-inch pieces and one with 10-inch pieces. Kits include the plates, screws, and other hardware needed to complete the frame. Price depends on size, with an 8 x 10 frame costing around $22.

WOODEN MOLDING

If you wish to build your own frame, you can use wooden molding like that sold in home-improvement warehouses for cabinets and flooring, or you can purchase picture frame molding from framing suppliers. An 8-foot length of molding will cost between $8 and $16. Look for molding with a groove deep enough to hold the glass and matted artwork. Often, you can buy molding pre-stained, pre-painted, or pre-finished, making it a very simple task to put together and touch up the frame.

SCREWDRIVER
You will need a slot-tip screwdriver to build a metal frame.

HAMMER
You can use a regular claw hammer, a balpeen hammer, or a smaller tack hammer for frame building. The smaller and more delicate the frame, the lighter the hammer you should use.

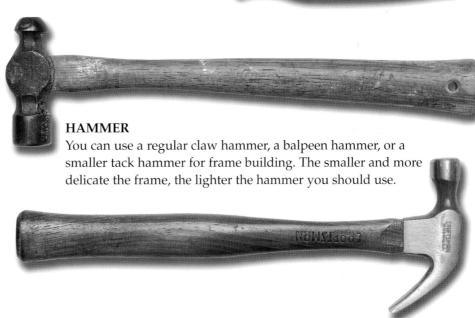

NAIL SET
This tool allows you to sink the nails in your wooden frame below the surface of the wood, hiding them from sight.

WOOD GLUE
Used to hold wooden frames together.

NAILS
Nails are used in wooden frames to keep the artwork and mount securely within the frame.

TOUCH-UP PENS
These pens are used to hide lighter areas or spots that might give a chipped appearance to the finished frame. They come in a variety of shades, so matching the frame's stain or paint shade isn't difficult. They can be found at art supply stores and some home-improvement retailers in the paint section.

TABLETOP MITER SAW

This type of saw allows for the cutting of corners at an angle, making it possible to build frames with snug, mitered corners. Power saws like the one shown cost around $150 to $200. A miter box—the part of the tabletop saw that allows for angled cuts—and handsaw can be purchased for around $100. Handsaws tend to be harder to use, and they can leave chipped, rough corners. If you don't plan to do enough woodworking to justify buying a saw, many lumber supply and home-improvement stores will cut molding to size for you for a nominal cost. Some craft stores and picture-framing professionals will do the same, also for a fee.

WOOD PUTTY AND PUTTY KNIFE

You will need to fill the small nail holes in your frame. Wood putty comes in a variety of colors, so you can match just about any shade you choose. The putty knife makes getting a smooth finished surface easy.

SAFETY GOGGLES

If you are going to use a miter saw or cut your own glass, you'll need appropriate eye protection.

OFFSETS

Framed and stretched canvasses are often thicker than the frame in which they are placed. In order to avoid damaging a canvas when securing it into the frame, offset fasteners like these are used. They are screwed into the frame and hold the canvas in place. They cost around $4 for a pack of 25 and are available in picture-framing supply shops.

PLIERS/WIRE CUTTERS

Useful for straightening nails or glazing points, screwing in hanging hardware, and dealing with wire.

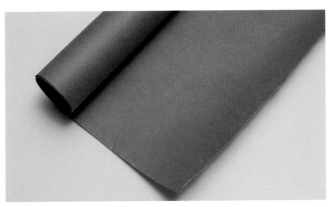

BACKING PAPER/DUST-COVER PAPER

Available at framing supply stores, this simple brown paper is placed over the back of the framed artwork and secured into place to keep dust and dirt out of the finished frame. Specific brands may or may not be acid-free. The paper comes in packs of sheets or in larger rolls. A pack of 25 sheets of acid-free 16 x 20-inch paper costs around $12. The rolls are more expensive, with a 300-foot roll costing about $40.

GLAZING POINTS

Used to secure the backing material and matted artwork into place inside the frame, glazing points come in a variety of sizes and are easily driven into softer woods with a screwdriver or small tack hammer. They can be found at hardware stores for $6 per package of a couple hundred points.

BRAD GUN/POINT DRIVER

Functions like a staple gun to shoot glazing points or brads into place along the inside edge of a picture frame. If you plan to do a lot of framing, you may want to purchase one. It can be found for around $40 at a hardware or home-improvement store. More expensive versions are available through online framing suppliers.

MARKING PEN

Used when cutting glass for drawing the lines directly onto the glass where you will need to score it.

11

GLASS

It is possible to get custom-cut sheets of glass inexpensively at hardware stores, picture-framing shops, and custom glass shops. Because of its ready availability and reasonable cost, we recommend purchasing your framing glass already cut. This eliminates the need to find safe storage space for large sheets of uncut glass, the dangers associated with trying to cut your own large sheet to size, and the resultant glass-shard dust that comes with hand-cutting glass. (You will still need to handle your piece of cut glass very carefully—never pick it up by the edges.) You should be able to purchase a small piece for a picture frame for around $8.

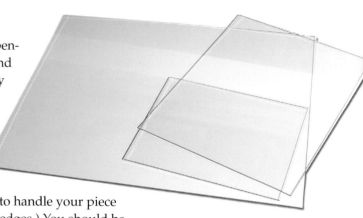

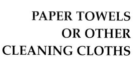

TOWEL

Use an old towel to cushion the glass while you clean and prepare it to go into the frame. It will protect the glass from the floor, and your hands from the glass.

GLASS CLEANER

Used to remove dirt and smudging from the glass before it goes into the frame.

PAPER TOWELS OR OTHER CLEANING CLOTHS

Before putting the glass into the frame, you need to make sure it is spotless. Any marks or dust will show up against the mat and mar the final effect.

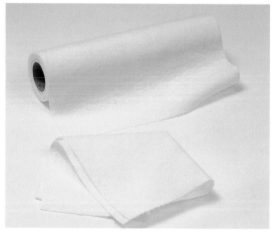

GLASS CUTTER

A simple glass cutter can be purchased at any hardware store or glass shop for around $4. More advanced ones can also be found, but they are more expensive. They are used to score the glass, which is then snapped along the cut.

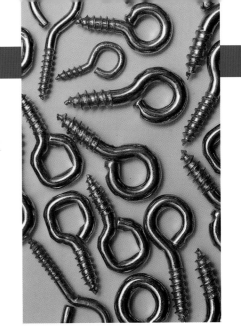

SCREW EYES

Screwed into the back of a finished picture frame and strung with wire for hanging, these screws come in a variety of sizes and with round or square holes. Available at hardware and home-improvement stores and anywhere else that picture-framing supplies are sold, they are inexpensive: a pack of 200, which will allow you to complete many projects, costs around $4.

HANGING WIRE

The final stage of preparing your framing project for display is to attach a strong wire to the hanging hardware. Sold in art supply stores and wherever else framing supplies are sold, rolls of wire come in a variety of lengths. You can purchase enough for many framing projects for around $4 or $5.

SAWTOOTH HANGERS

Sawtooth hangers are attached to the frame at the top edge, with the teeth pointing toward the bottom of the piece. Most sawtooth hangers have a small dot marking the center point. Some can be embedded directly into the frame, while others require the use of small nails to affix them to the frame. They cannot be used on large or heavy pieces but are ideal for smaller framing projects where you don't want to use wire. A pack of 25 hangers costs around $2.

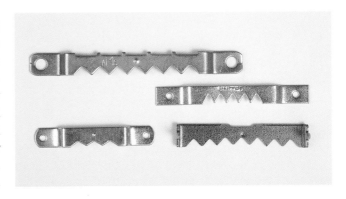

PICTURE HANGERS

Small metal hooks with a loop at the top for a nail to be driven in, these hangers protect the wall surface by providing a space between the head of the nail and the wall itself. They can be found at frame shops, home-improvement stores, and most hardware stores, and they are not expensive.

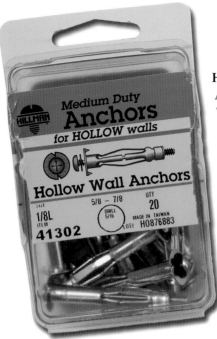

HOLLOW WALL ANCHORS

Also called molly bolts, wall anchors are useful for hanging heavy items. They consist of a fitted sleeve with an internal screw. The sleeve is inserted into the wall, and the screw is tightened and then unscrewed far enough to accommodate the loop of the hanger or the wire. The sleeve provides extra gripping power inside the wall. Anchors are not easily reversible, so they are generally not used with smaller or lighter frames.

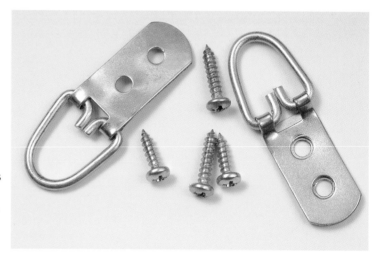

MIRROR HANGERS

Loops of metal secured with two or more screws into the back of either side of the frame, mirror hangers provide more support than either a single-attachment hanger such as a sawtooth or a wire strung across the back of a frame. They are used for hanging large or heavy frames. A pack of 20 costs around $30.

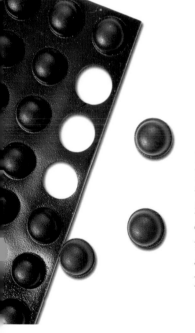

BUMP-ONS

Bump-ons are small rubber nubs that have adhesive backing and are secured onto the bottom corners of the back of the frame. They protect both the wall and the frame, allow for air circulation behind the frame, and act to stabilize the bottom edge of the piece so it is less likely to move right or left and look crooked on the wall. Packets of sheets are available at art supply and framing supply shops for around $4. Since you really need only two per piece, no matter how large, a single packet will provide enough for many framing projects.

CARPENTER'S LEVEL

A level makes it possible to hang artwork straight, even when mirror hangers are used, by ensuring that the hangers are aligned horizontally and vertically according to your measurements.

2
Matting

Sizing the Mat

The hardest part of any matting job is determining the size of the mat you want to use. You need to determine all measurements before cutting anything. A good rule of thumb is "Measure twice, cut once."

First, measure the height and width of the image area to be framed. If the edges of the image will be cov-ered by the mat, it is standard to have a $\frac{1}{8}$-inch overlay on each side, so you will need to subtract $\frac{1}{4}$ inch from both the height and width. For example, a 5 x 7 piece with a standard overlay of $\frac{1}{8}$ inch will have working measurements of $4\frac{3}{4}$ x $6\frac{3}{4}$. This will be the size of the window you will cut into the mat.

Next, determine the size of the mat border you want to use. Ultimately, the decision about which dimensions for a mat make the most pleasing display of the artwork is based on individual preference. While standard sizes do exist (see the chart below), rigid rules regarding mat widths have given way in recent years to a more experimental approach. For example, it was once unheard of for a small piece to be placed in a large frame with a wide mat, but that look can be very appealing and is more common today. (However, if you are using a standard-size frame, your mat size should match it.)

As with other aesthetic aspects of matting, experimentation is the best way to figure out what you like. Look around at framed artwork and pay attention to the matting as well as the piece itself. When doing your own framing, try out different mat widths to see what

appeals to you. Just keep in mind that a very narrow border can make an image look crowded into the frame, while a very wide border can make the image seem lost or overshadowed by the mat.

Add the width of the mat you select to the length of each of the image window's four sides. For a 5 x 7 image with window measurements of $4^3/4 \times 6^3/4$ and a $1^5/8$-inch mat width, you would add $1^5/8$ inches to each side, or $3^1/4$ inches ($1^5/8 \times 2$) to the window's length and width, giving 8 x 10 as the measurements for the entire piece. You would need to cut a mat that matches these outer dimensions and then cut the interior window.

If you are using a pre-made frame, you must be able to match the frame dimensions while leaving adequate space for matting around the work, so do the calculations before you buy the frame.

Standard Image Sizes and Border Widths (in inches)

Image Dimensions	Border Width
5 x 7	$1^1/2$
8 x 10	2
11 x 14	2
16 x 20	$2^1/2$
18 x 24	$2^1/2$
20 x 24	3
22 x 28	3
24 x 30	$3^1/2$
24 x 36	$3^1/2$
26 x 32	$3^1/2$
30 x 40	4
32 x 40	4

The Bottom Border

It was conventional for many years to add additional width to the bottom border of the mat. This additional space makes the mat appear more balanced to the eye when the artwork is viewed from a lower vantage point. Today, it is no longer considered standard, although if you are planning to place the framed piece high on a wall, you might wish to add the extra width. If you do so, the standard extra width is $1/4$ to $1/2$ inch added to the bottom border only and figured into your measurements. For very small frames, the extra space may result in a more crowded-looking image, and for most conventional hanging arrangements, where the art is placed around eye level, it isn't necessary at all.

Selecting the Matboard

Matboards are available in a tremendous variety of colors and textures, which can make choosing one for your project seem like an overwhelming task. Simply choosing a white mat can involve sorting through several different shades, from "white" white to "arctic" white to tones of off-white and ivory. Coupled with this we selection of color is the fact that most advice on matting states that you should stick with neutral colors—shades of white and gray—to avoid making the wrong color choice. It is true that neutral tones work well for pieces such as black and white photographs or when you want the entire focus to be on the piece framed, with no distraction from the mat. (Most of the photographs, drawings, and prints you see in art galleries have "white" white mats.) It is also true that a colored mat can clash with a decorating scheme and a little more care will need to be taken in planning and placement to avoid this possibility. But don't be afraid to experiment with color when planning your mats. Color can greatly enhance the artwork and the frame and bring an overall appeal to the final product that might be lacking with a neutral, off-white, or gray mat. Just keep in mind a few basic tips when deciding on the use of color in your mat.

- Lighter mats take your eye out of the frame and render the artwork more "open" to its surroundings. Darker mats keep your eye in the frame, boxing in the artwork and setting it apart. (Neither of these is necessarily a bad thing; it's again mostly a matter of what you are framing and your personal preference.)
- A photograph matted in white looks a bit different from the same photograph matted in gray or black. Black and white photographs actually contain a multitude of shades of gray. This can be clearly illustrated by placing the same photograph into a black mat, a white mat, and a gray mat.

Neutral tones work best for black and white photographs. They're also the least likely to draw attention from the framed work.

The white mat has a stark appearance, bringing more prominence to the lighter elements with the frame.

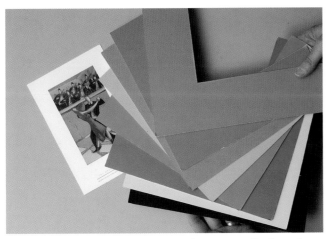

Well-chosen mat colors can make a frame more lively and interesting while complementing the subject.

A black mat brings out the darker tones and closes in the frame.

The gray mat balances the tones of the photo. It closes in the frame, but not as strongly as the black mat.

- A color print matted in a neutral shade of white or gray looks significantly different from the same colors done with a black mat or with a colorful double or triple mat.

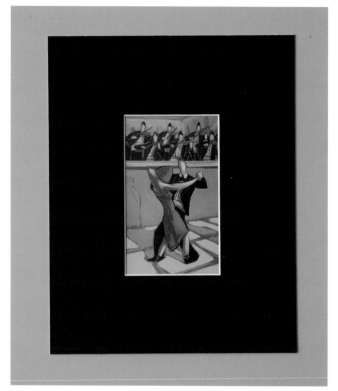

The darker mat closes the artwork in and brings the focus more to the center of the picture. It also subtly enhances the play of color within the piece, making the brighter tones stand out a bit more while bringing out the darker shadows.

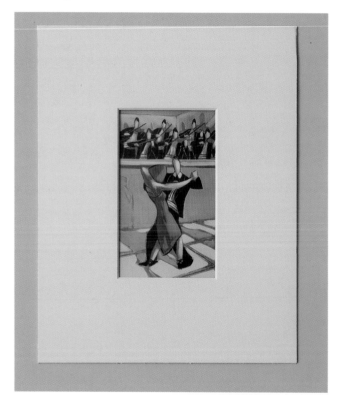

The lighter mat brings the eye out of the frame and lets the colors within the picture speak for themselves.

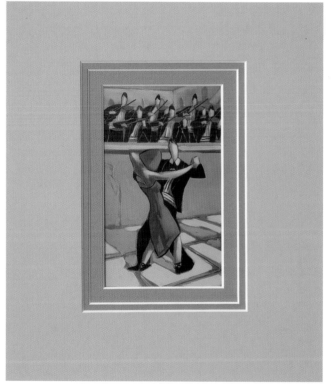

A double or triple mat allows for more creativity in the choice of mat colors and can enhance several elements within the piece at once.

Look at matted and framed artwork in galleries and shops and homes to get an idea what appeals to you in terms of color; note what you think works and what doesn't.

Most places that sell matboard have corners of each color and type of matboard they sell, which allow you to get an idea what the mat will look like when placed against the work you intend to frame. If possible, take the piece you wish to mat with you when you go to buy matboard and spend some time playing with different colors and layers.

Try some of the white mats, then some of the darker grays. Look at the piece you wish to frame—try to find the subtle colors within it and find mats that enhance those tones. Try some bolder colors and see if you think it overwhelms the artwork or adds to it. Above all, have fun experimenting. Practice and experience will give you a better eye for the subtleties of mat color and as time goes on, you might find your choices getting richer and more complex.

The same goes for textures. Matboards come in a variety of textures, although the more unusual ones might only be available at frame shops or specialty stores rather than the local art supply shop. Subtle textures can add interest and depth to a mat and complement the elements of the piece being framed. More dramatic textures can be a distraction, or they can add an element of boldness to a work. Again, look around at what is available, develop a sense for what appeals to you and what doesn't, and start with more subtle textures before getting into the bolder ones.

Try out both light and dark shades when deciding on a mat color.

A good mat color often brings out subtle colors within the subject.

Cutting the Outer Border

For this example, we used a mat with an outside measurement of 8 x 10 inches. The corners of the large sheets you purchase at framing supply shops are generally square. When you begin to cut the mat, it's easiest to start with one of the corners of a large matboard so you will only have to make two cuts. You begin by laying the mat facedown on a non-slip surface. Make sure the surface is clean so that you don't mar the mat when you place it down.

1. Measure 8 inches along one edge of the matboard and make a small pencil mark. Turn the matboard 90 degrees, measure 10 inches along that side, and make another small pencil mark. These marks indicate where you need to place the edge of the T-square to draw your cutting lines.

2. Align the T-square and draw the first line.

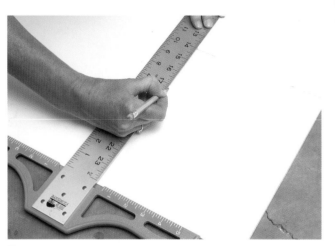

3. Then turn the board 90 degrees and draw the second line.

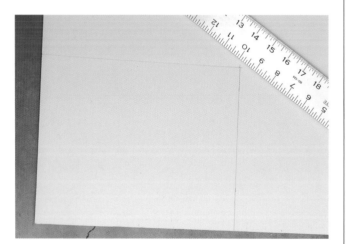

You should now have two intersecting pencil lines showing the edges of the matboard you want to cut.

4. Place the matboard facedown on a cutting surface. This surface should be solid and flat and large enough to allow you to make one smooth cut for each side. If your tabletop workspace is not large enough, you can use the floor. Place a clean protective layer between your matboard and the floor or tabletop. A clean piece of cardboard is ideal, because it will cushion the tip of the blade as you cut through the matboard. It will also make the edges of the cut neater and less likely to feather or tear.

5. Place a metal straight edge with a non-slip backing along one of the pencil lines. It should be long enough to cover the whole line.

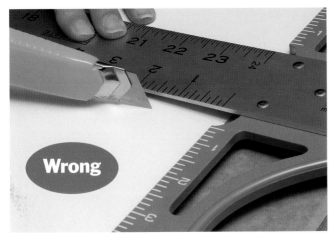

Wrong

The T-square will not work well for cutting, because when placed flat on a surface, there will be a gap between the matboard you wish to cut and the top of the T-square. It is much easier to use a ruler.

6. Now cut the edges of the mat using a sharp utility knife. Dull blades tend to slip and to make ragged cuts, so test the sharpness before you begin. Change the blade often when cutting multiple mats, before it becomes too dull and ruins your work. Once you have a sharp blade attached, place the edge of the knife against the straight edge and use a firm pressure to cut through the matboard.

As you cut, hold the ruler firmly and press down so it doesn't slip. After you have made the cut, keep the ruler in place and lift the cut-away piece slightly to see if you have cut all the way through. You may need to make another cut to get through the matboard. Don't move the ruler until you are certain you have cut through— repositioning the ruler to make a second cut accurately is very difficult.

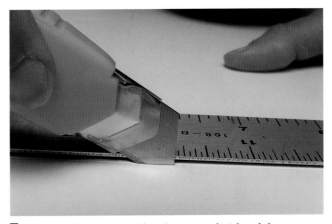

7. Repeat this process for the second side of the mat.

After you have cut both sides of the mat, you should have an 8 x 10-inch piece of matboard with four 90-degree corners and smooth, straight edges. You are now ready to cut the interior window.

Using a Handheld Cutter

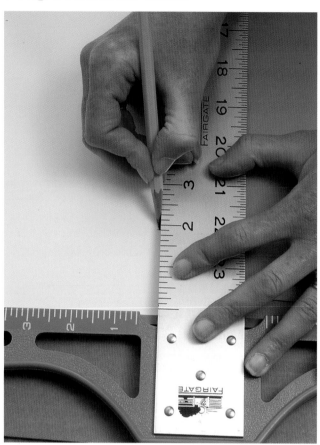

1. To cut a $4^3/_4$ x $6^3/_4$-inch window into the mat with a handheld cutter, you must first mark the outline of the window onto the back of the matboard. Place the mat facedown on a clean surface and use your T-square to measure in the width of your borders (in this case, $1^5/_8$ inches) from each edge of the board and make a mark with your pencil on each side.

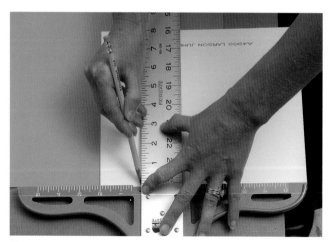

2. Then use the T-square and pencil to connect the marks . . .

. . . and outline the window to be cut.

3. Circle the corners with your pencil so you can see them while you are cutting. This will help you avoid overcutting the corners.

Matting

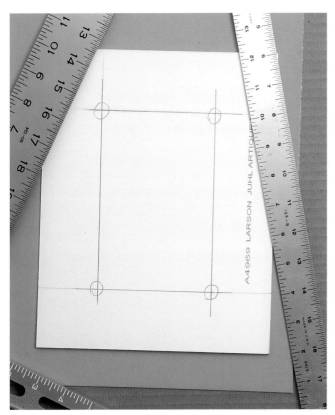

4. *Always* double-check your measurements before you begin cutting.

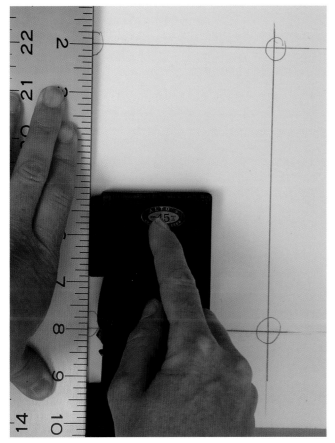

5. You are now ready to use the handheld cutter. After you've adjusted the blade (see sidebar), place the mat facedown on a slipsheet so that you can see the pencil

marks you have made. Move the straight edge until the pencil line is positioned precisely along its right side. (Always keep the window to the right side of your straight edge. This will ensure that the bevel is properly cut all around. The strips of mat that will eventually be seen with your artwork should be under the ruler when you are cutting.) With the ruler in position, you can then place the cutter alongside it.

Adjusting a Handheld Cutter

The blade of the mat cutter is adjustable, so you have to make sure you have it set to the proper depth before beginning your cut. Test-cut a scrap piece of mat on a hard, flat surface with a slipsheet of similar scrap underneath. The top piece of scrap should be easily cut through on one pass with a light score mark left on the bottom piece. If it is too shallow, you won't get a complete cut on the first pass; if it is too deep, the blade will cut into the lower surface and drag, resulting in a ragged or crooked cut. Blade depth is very important for a good-quality mat. Experiment until you know the proper feel for the thickness of matboard you are working with, and remember that you will need to adjust the blade depth again if you change the blade or switch to a different type of matboard.

6. You will need to check the blade of your mat cutter to see how much space there will be between the blade and the edge of your ruler. Because of the way they are designed, most mat cutters have about $1/8$ inch between the edge where the cutter will slide along the ruler and where the blade will bite into the mat. This means that if you simply run the mat cutter along the ruler while holding it down along the penciled line, your cut will be $1/8$ inch off.

Some mat cutters make allowances for this gap, and the Alto's 45 mat cutter shown here is one of them. By adding a slight groove to the side of the cutter you run along the ruler, the manufacturers have eliminated the need to figure out the offset. If you do not have this feature on your mat cutter, you will need to do a test cut on some scrap mat to determine how far to the left of your pencil line you need to align your ruler. Everything must be positioned so that the blade enters the board at exactly the proper spot.

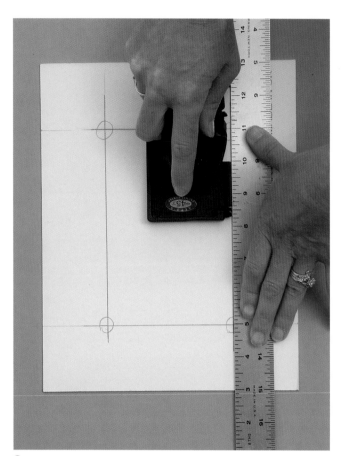

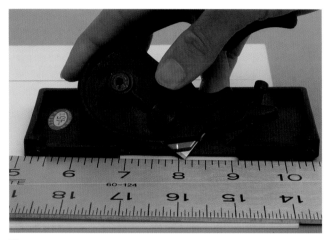

7. The blade will not cut completely through the mat until about $1/8$ inch into the cut, and you must allow for this by starting the cut approximately $1/8$ inch beyond where you want the finished window to begin.

8. Holding the ruler firmly in place with your left hand, place the left edge of the mat cutter lightly against the right edge of the ruler. Check to make sure the blade will begin cutting in the right place, which in this case is $1/8$ inch below the corner.

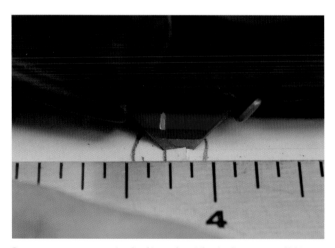

Some mat cutters, including the Alto's, have small lines on either side of the blade, showing you where to start and where to finish your cut. If yours does not, you will need to practice a bit until you know where along the line to start and finish your cut.

9. Hold the mat cutter firmly and lower it, letting the blade penetrate the board.

10. Push the cutter away from you along the ruler's edge. Don't push down too hard—a firm, steady pressure works best.

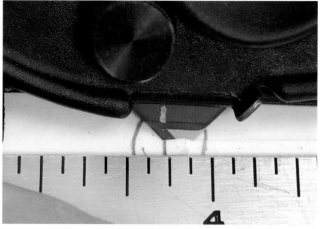

11. When the blade has reached your penciled circle at the corner, stop and lift the blade clear. The cut should extend to the penciled corner of the box but not beyond.

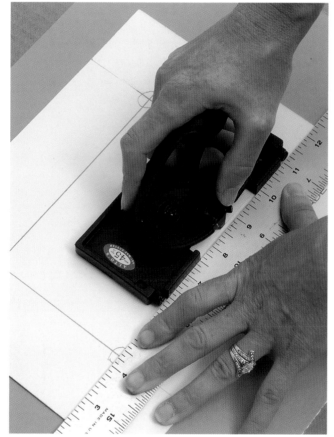

Keep the ruler firmly in place as you cut the length of your pencil line.

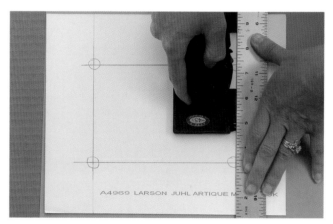

12. To make the next cut, lift your straight edge and reposition the mat so that the pencil line that was at the top is now along the ruler's edge. Remember to keep the window you are cutting to the right of the ruler and the strip of the border underneath it in order to keep the bevel angle correct. Again, position the blade carefully so that the blade starts its cut at the proper spot. Cut with a firm, smooth stroke.

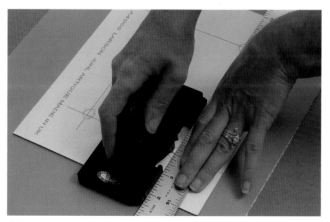

13. Repeat this process with the remaining sides of your mat.

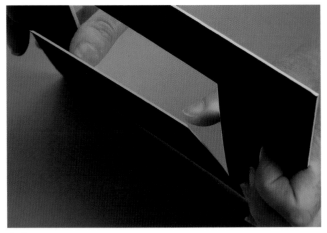

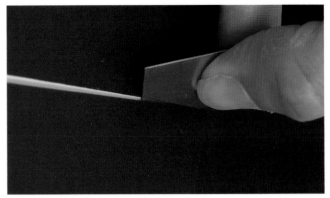

14. When you've made four cuts, the hole should fall clear . . .

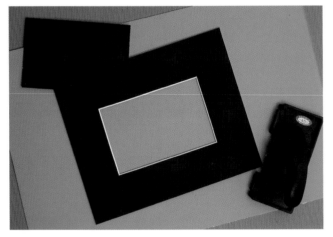

. . . and you should be left with a cleanly cut board.

This should give you a clean cut, but if any small tears hang in the corners, you can gently rub them away with an emery board. It's better to slightly undercut the corners than to overcut them. The tiny overlapping lines on overcut corners tend to worsen with time, and as the damage progresses, they become more visible in the mat.

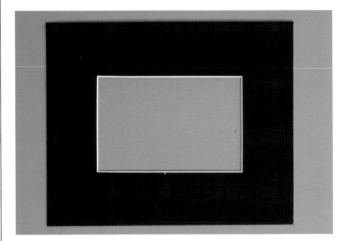

16. You can rub the inside of the beveled edges of a cut matboard very lightly with a clean cloth or an artist's kneaded eraser to eliminate any tiny frays left by the cutting. If the cut is ragged, you were probably working with a dull blade and should change it before doing any further cutting.

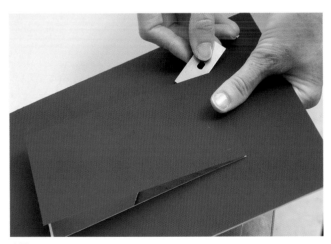

15. If the hole does not quite drop away because you undercut your mat window on one or more corners, pick up the mat and turn it so the front side is facing you. Carefully slide a single-edge razor blade into the cut, matching the angle of the bevel, and use a gentle sawing motion to cut through the rest of the mat.

Practice Makes Perfect

The best way to improve your skill at cutting precise mats with relative ease is to practice on scraps. Ask at framer's shops if they sell or give away scraps. (When you're cutting, it's a good idea to keep scrap pieces handy anyway, to put underneath good pieces and to test the sharpness of your blade before you begin cutting out a mat.) Practice cutting mats until you can determine where the blade will sink into the mat, how far from your penciled line the straight edge has to be in order for the blade to precisely follow the line, and where to stop the blade to get well-cut corners.

Using a Tabletop Cutter

A tabletop mat cutting system is an alternative to a handheld mat cutter. While more expensive than a handheld cutter, tabletop systems have certain advantages. With adjustable border-width systems and simple blade replacement, tabletop cutters can make smooth work of cutting a variety of mat sizes. Overcutting and cutting crooked lines are less of a problem with a tabletop cutter as well, because you aren't relying on your own attention to hold the straight edge in place. The disadvantages of the tabletop cutter are the cost and the fact that the size of mat you can cut is limited by the size of the cutter you purchase. If you buy a small tabletop cutter to get started, you will not be able to cut larger mats with it. This might not be a problem if you never intend to frame anything beyond the capability of the system.

You begin by determining the mat's border widths and setting the cutter margins to match. Border widths are determined the same way as for a handheld cutter, but the tabletop mat cutter will make measuring and marking easier. In this example, we cut an 11 x 14-inch outer border around a 5 x 7-inch image with a $1/4$-inch total overlap. This gave us a window size of $4^{1}/_{4}$ x $6^{1}/_{4}$, a mat border width of $3^{3}/_{8}$, and a border height of $3^{3}/_{8}$ at the top. For demonstration purposes, we added some extra width to the bottom, for a bottom border width of $4^{3}/_{8}$ inches.

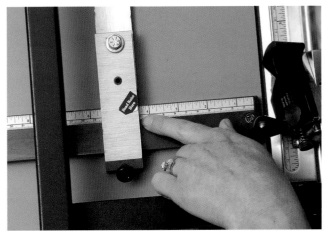

1. To mark the mat, you must first set the measurements on your tabletop cutter. This means simply moving the bar to the proper place along the ruler at the base and tightening the screws to hold it in place. Set the mat facedown and, sliding it under the cutting arm, align it so it fits snugly into the corner formed by the measuring arms of the cutter.

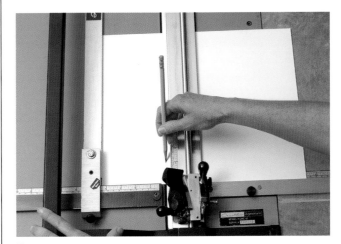

2. Use a sharp pencil to draw your lines. It is easiest to mark the height on one side and then turn the mat 180 degrees to mark the height on the other side.

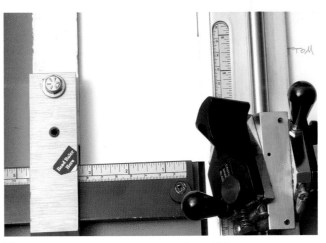

3. Reset the cutter to measure the width.

4. Mark both sides along the width of the mat.

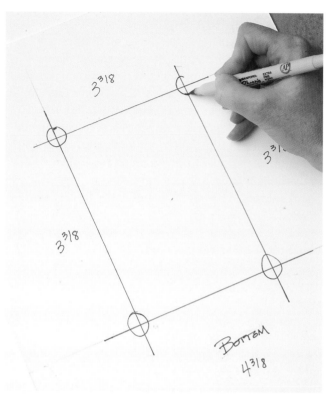

6. Recheck your measurements to be sure they are correct, and circle the corners where the lines intersect to make it easier to see them while you are cutting.

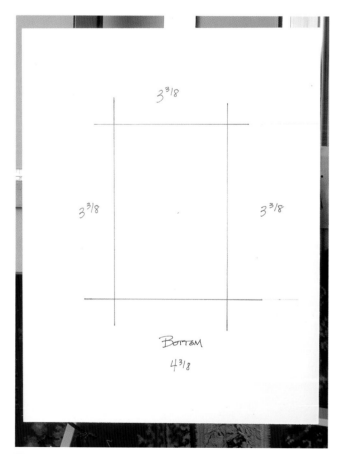

5. When you are finished, you will have the window drawn on the back of the mat.

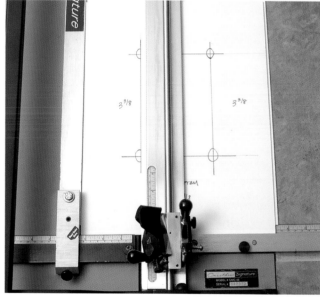

7. You are now ready to cut your mat. Reset the left stop bar of the mat cutter and place a slipsheet of scrap matboard under the workspace. The slipsheet should be slightly longer than the longest cut you will make; otherwise, your blade will not make a smooth cut when it overruns the slipsheet. Place the marked mat into position on top of the slipsheet so that the pencil line is aligned with the cutter bar and with the mat window to the right. This will keep the bevel consistent for all four sides of your mat.

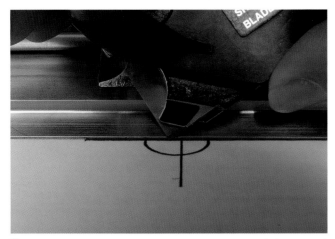

8. Position the cutter at the bottom corner of the pencil outline. Most cutters are marked near the blade with two small lines, one to show where to start the cut, and one to show where to finish the cut in order to have evenly cut corners. You should experiment with scrap mat in order to determine how far below the corner to begin the cut and where to end it.

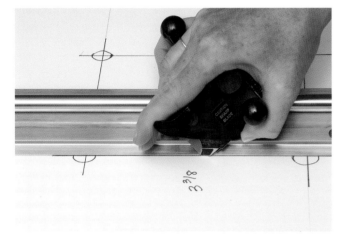

9. When the cutter is positioned properly, simply press down with a firm, steady pressure and push the cutter away from you along the bar. The result should be a neat, straight cut. If you don't get a clean cut, you probably need to change a dull blade.

10. Turn the mat 90 degrees and reset the measurements for the next side.

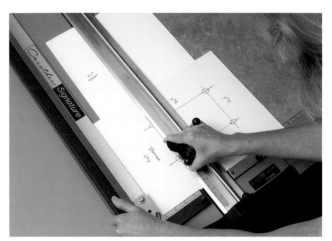

11. Reposition the blade at the bottom of the cutter bar and cut the second side.

It is best when cutting to reset the bar each time and turn the matboard 90 degrees so that the side you just cut is at the bottom of the workspace and you are proceeding from a cut corner to an uncut one. (The exception is the final side, where you go from one cut corner to another.)

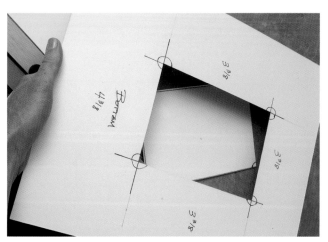

12. When you have completed all four sides, the mat window should fall clear.

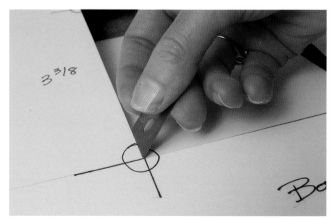

13. If it does not, use a single-edged razor blade to gently cut it free, being sure to follow the bevel of the cut. Check the window to be sure there are no small tears or pieces of torn mat hanging from the edges. These are signs of a dull blade, and you can gently rub them away with an emery board or soft eraser. Do not pull on them, which can make the tear worse and damage the edge of your window.

Curved and Oval Mats

Making oval mats requires the purchase of a template system with a blade that moves in the appropriate pattern. These are generally quite expensive for the beginner, starting at around $100. For far less than that, you can instead have these mats custom-cut at framing shops, craft shops, and most other places that do picture framing or sell the supplies. Unless you are going to be doing a lot of oval matting, the oval cutters are generally not a good investment.

Cutting curved lines in mats can add a decorative touch to them, but it is not a project for a beginner. You either must trace the edge of a curved object or ruler to get the proper shape or you must cut freehand. Regular handheld mat cutters are difficult to use for this purpose because they are made to cut straight lines, and the blade is usually placed in the middle of the tool, making it hard to maneuver. It is also difficult to trace around curved objects with a straight-edged handheld mat cutter. Special mat cutters with the blades positioned at the front are available; these make freehand cutting easier, but much practice is still required to learn the skill. If you would like to try curved mats, the best advice is to practice and become skilled at cutting square mats, then purchase a mat cutter with the blade at the front edge before you move on to attempting curves.

side than the top mat. This will allow the double mat to fit more easily into the rabbeted frame, which might not be wide enough to accommodate two widths of matboard. Cut the outside borders to size for both mats.

In addition to deciding how wide you want the mat border to be, you must choose how much of the bottom mat you want to show. It is fairly standard for the reveal on a double mat to be $1/4$ to $1/2$ inch wide. If it is too wide, it takes over the image, while if it is very narrow, it won't make an impact on the eye. Experiment with mats or go look at examples of framed, double-matted work to get an idea what appeals to you. The top window is measured to allow for the image size plus the reveal on each side, while the bottom window is figured the same as for a single mat—the total size of the piece you are framing minus the overlap added to each side.

For a 5 x 7-inch image with an overlap of $1/8$ inch on each side (leaving an image size and bottom mat window measurement of $4^3/4$ x $6^3/4$ inches) and a $1/4$-inch-wide reveal, you would add $1/4$ inch to the length of each side of the image. In practice, this means adding $1/2$ inch to the length and width, which will give you a top window measurement of $5^1/4$ x $7^1/4$ inches.

Double Mats

Double matting, in which a top-layer matboard is cut with a slightly wider window than an underlying matboard, can add interest and contrast to the frame. It can also provide additional space between the artwork and the glass of the frame.

The confusing thing about cutting double mats is that the top mat (the mat that will be most visible from the front of the finished mat) is going to be the *bottom* mat when you have it turned over so that you can mark and cut from the back. The bottom mat, which will be visible from the front of the finished mat as a thin strip of contrasting or complementary color—called a reveal—showing underneath the top mat, will actually be on the *top* when you are working on marking and cutting. It might help to actually write "Top" and "Bottom" on the backs of the matboards so that you can keep that in mind when you're working, or to think of them as the front and back rather than top and bottom mats. (Note that the word "bottom" on the backs of the photographed mats in this section refers to the vertical bottom of a mat, not to which mat is in front of or behind another.)

For double mats, you determine the outer measurements the same way you would for a single mat, except the bottom mat should be about $1/8$ inch shorter on each

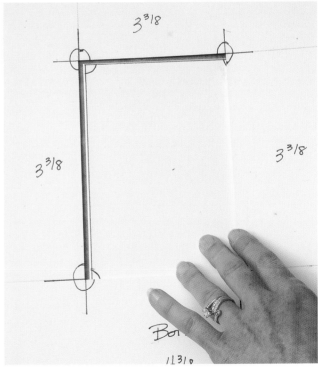

1. In this example, we use a tabletop mat cutter. You begin by marking and cutting the top mat as described in the previous section. When you have your top mat cut and the window has fallen clear, place the mat back together.

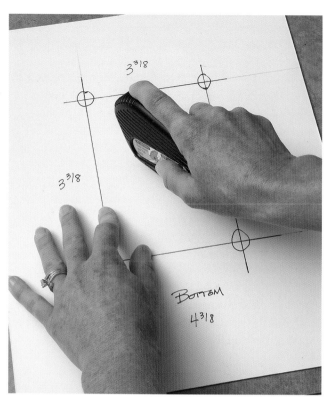

2. Using acid-free double-sided tape, place a line of adhesive along each edge of the cut mat and inside the cutout mat window.

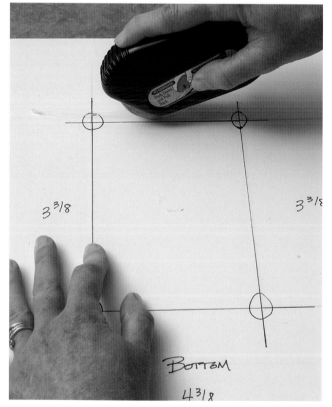

Keep the tape inside the window, close to the cut you have made but not over it. Adhesive placed over the cuts will show in the mat window when you remove the cutout window.

If you do run over the lines and across the cut with your adhesive, simply rub it away with your fingertips.

3. Take your bottom mat and align it with your cut mat.

32

4. Place it down and gently pound on it over the adhesive to make sure you get a good seal.

5. It may be helpful at this point to mark your measurements onto the back of the mat, to make it easier to remember what you are doing, but it isn't necessary and is done here for demonstration purposes.

6. Mark the new measurements onto the back of the mat just as you did for the single mat (see page 22).

7. Cut the mat as you did before, turning and resetting the measurements for each side. You will not need a slipsheet for cutting the mat now, because the top mat provides the necessary cushion to protect the blade.

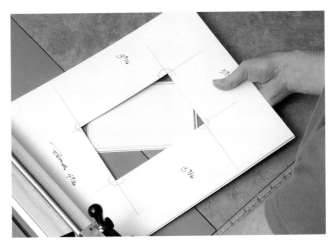

8. When you are finished, the center window will again drop free.

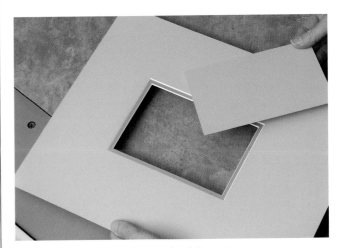

You now have a neatly cut double mat.

Triple Mats

Triple mats are easy to do once you have the skills to complete a double mat, and they can broaden the possibilities for choosing colors to use with your artwork.

To make a triple mat, it's easiest to figure out the inner window first. That will have the smallest dimensions you can use while still allowing your framed piece to show properly. Then calculate the dimensions for the middle and front-mat windows based on how much of those mats you want to be visible from the front.

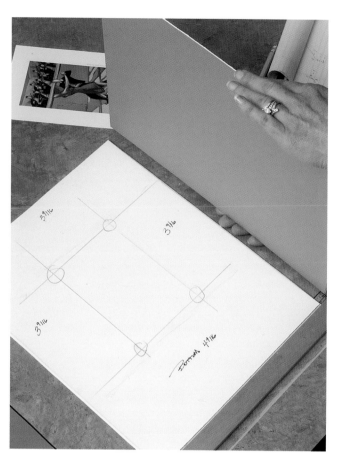

3. Take the new bottom mat . . .

1. Place the cutout window piece back into the center of your double mat.

2. Apply acid-free double-sided tape along the cuts and on the back of the window piece.

. . . and align it with the double mat.

34

4. Gently pound on the third mat to anchor it into place.

5. Measure and mark each of the sides of the new window.

6. Cut the third mat window.

7. When you are finished, the window will again fall clear . . .

. . . and you will have a completed triple mat (shown here with the image in the window.)

3

Mounting

Mounting artwork is simply the process of affixing the art in place so that it can then be framed and displayed. In most cases, if properly done, the actual mounting materials will be hidden by the artwork or the matting and won't be visible in the final framed product. Because the mounting materials come into contact with the artwork, acid-free materials are recommended, especially if you are mounting something of value. Most methods, with the exception of spray mounting, are also reversible, which means that they can be removed from the artwork without causing damage. Before deciding on how to mount your artwork, consider carefully how valuable the piece is to you, how long you want the framing job to endure, and whether or not you want the option of reversing the process at some point in the future. For example, a delicate watercolor should not be mounted with materials that are only reversible with water, since applying water to the painting will damage it.

Foam board makes excellent backing material for most framing projects. It is available at art supply shops and wherever else matboard is sold. It can be used for matting, and comes in a variety of colors for that purpose, but its main function is as supportive backing. The foam board will be cut to the same size as the matboard you are using for the project, following the same techniques outlined for cutting the matboard to size in the previous chapter. On a flat surface large enough to accommodate the project, you simply measure with your T-square, draw pencil lines to indicate the borders of the piece, and then cut out the backing, using your straight edge to guide the blade of your knife so you get a good clean cut. The coreboard is generally a bit thicker than matboard, so you may have to follow the cut two or three times to get through. Be sure your blade is sharp.

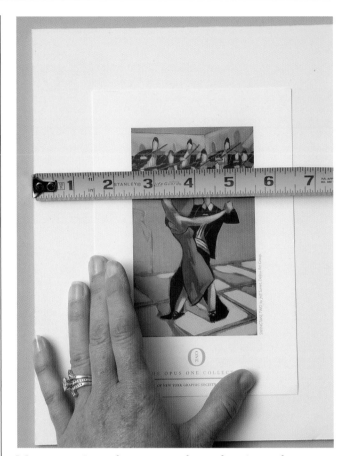

Measure twice to be sure you have the piece where you want it.

1. After you've cut the foam board, the next step is to determine where to place the art. The easiest way to do that is to use your tape measure to determine where the mat borders fall and place the artwork within them.

Mounting

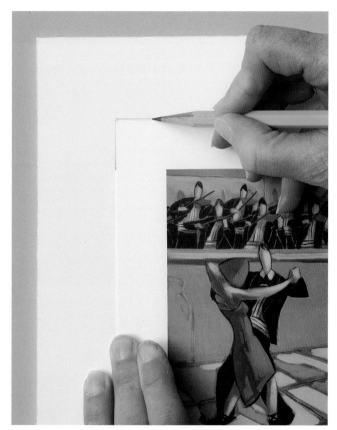

2. Make two or three small pencil marks along the edge of the piece on each side.

3. Tracing the image will most likely leave a graphite mark along the edge of the work, so don't do this if the piece has value or if you think you might want to frame it differently in the future and would like to have the option of allowing the edges to show. Instead, lift the artwork off the mountboard and use your straight edge to draw the solid outline of the piece, creating a box on the foam board.

You can mount the artwork to the backing using a variety of methods. The ones covered here are the most suitable for the beginner.

If the item you are framing is not particularly valuable, or if you are using an irreversible mounting method such as spraying, you can simply trace around the edge of the piece where it lies on the mountboard.

A T-hinge is simply two strips of adhesive material affixed in a T shape to hold the artwork to the mountboard. The hinges are placed evenly at the top of the piece about a third of the way in from either side. Their size will be determined by the size of the artwork. You will need at least two hinges per job. Larger artwork might require more in order to provide sufficient support, but they will still need to be spaced evenly. You can hang the artwork either on the mountboard or on the mat if the work is not large or heavy. T-hinges are easy to make and work well when the edges of the piece will be covered by the matboard.

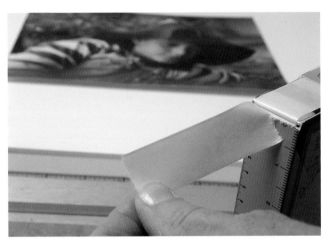

1. Cut two pieces of acid-free tape or Filmoplast per hinge.

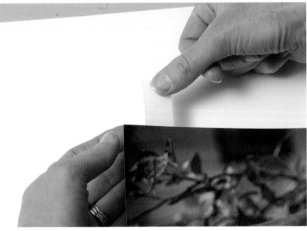

2. Place the artwork faceup on a clean, protected surface. Apply the first two strips of tape to the back of the piece at the top edge, with half the tape above the edge.

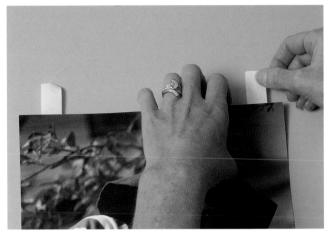

3. If you are affixing the work to the mountboard, place it within your marked border and use the burnisher to smooth the tape into place.

4. Tear or cut two more strips of tape and lay them across the first two pieces, forming a T.

5. Burnish them smooth as well.

6. You can, if you like, mark the back of the matboard instead of the foam board in order to place the art. You simply apply an additional piece of Filmoplast to each hinge to form a T, burnish the hinges into place, and lay the artwork and mat together onto the mountboard.

You then press down to affix the tape. Carefully lift the mat with the artwork attached and turn it over onto your work surface.

Other Types of Hinges

V-HINGES
V-hinging is an alternative method for mounting artwork and is especially effective when the edges of the work will be exposed rather than covered by the mat. Unlike T-hinges, V-hinges leave nothing showing when the art is viewed from the front.

To make a V-hinge, cut or tear two strips of tape for each hinge, as with a T-hinge. Place the artwork facedown on a clean work surface and then simply fold one piece of tape in half and apply half to the back of the artwork, keeping the other half folded back so it doesn't stick to your working surface. Attach a crosspiece to the top half of the tape—the part that protrudes above the artwork—with the adhesive side facing forward, in the same direction as the first piece. Then position the image on the mountboard and secure the crosspiece into place.

RICE PAPER HINGES
Rice-paper hinges were once the standard for conservation-quality mounting, and they are still used in some types of mounting and framing. They are created by combining rice paper with cooked rice starch, which acts as an adhesive in the mounting process. The starch comes in powder form and must be mixed with water and cooked in the microwave for about 20 seconds or so, until the gel becomes clear. The starch is then painted onto the paper with a small brush. Modern inks, dyes, and printing processes can interact badly with rice starch, causing discoloration of the dyes on artwork and on matboard. Thinner pieces, such as watercolors or paper documents, can be damaged by the moisture in the starch and can tear easily. The starch can dry out over time and lose its adhesive qualities. The process is also rather messy and requires a quick hand, because the paste mixture spoils quickly and requires monitoring. With the ready availability of acid-free tapes, Filmoplast, and other durable and safe alternative adhesives—none of which require the work or mess of preparing the starch—rice paper and starch have become obsolete for the home hobbyist.

Mounting

Adhesive corners like those used to hold photos in albums make good mounting materials for some artwork. Because they are designed for contact with photographs, acid-free varieties are available in craft stores, art supply shops, and wherever scrapbooking materials are sold. Check the packaging and make sure it says "acid-free" on it.

Choose a size that will be large enough to support the piece. The corners needn't be huge, however; they are designed to hold photographs, so you can judge from that the approximate size you will use. If in doubt, opt for a medium or larger size that can be trimmed down, rather than a tiny size that might not hold well.

It is best to affix all four corners to the artwork and then place it down on your marked mountboard. Placing each corner and anchoring it as you go will force you to bend and possibly wrinkle the artwork to get the last couple of corners.

. . . and slip it gently onto a corner of the piece.

2. Place the artwork down, carefully aligning the corners to match the pencil lines on the matboard.

1. Take each corner . . .

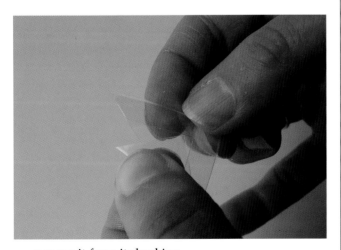

. . . remove it from its backing . . .

3. Press gently on each corner to affix it.

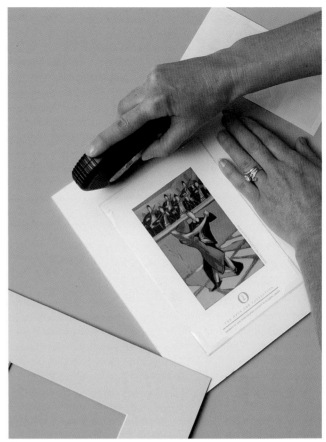

5. You can then use double-sided acid-free tape to join the matboard to the mountboard, since the adhesive does not come into contact with the artwork. Apply the tape to the mountboard around your piece on each side. Be careful *not* to let the tape touch the artwork. Place the matboard down and pound it gently to seal the adhesive.

4. Check to make sure the edges of the corners will not protrude from under the mat when it is laid on top of the artwork. If they do, you can trim them back with scissors, being very careful not to scratch or cut the artwork underneath.

Making Your Own Photo Corners

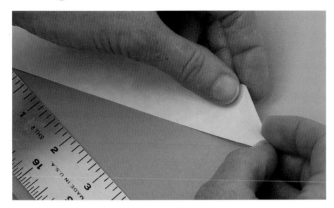

1. Start with a strip of acid-free paper, cut about an inch wide and several inches long. Use your utility knife or a pair of scissors to cut the strip and try to get it as even as possible in width. Fold one end down so that the vertical edge meets the bottom edge, forming a small triangle. This is one half of a corner.

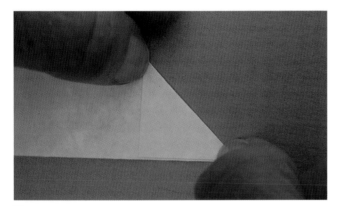

2. Crease the fold gently with your fingers, keeping the edges even across the bottom.

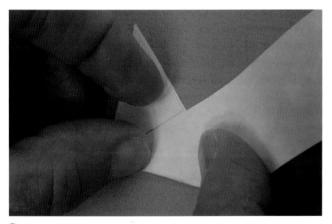

3. Now lift the folded end of the strip and fold it again to form the other half of the triangle. The top edge of the strip should meet the other half of the corner in the center of the triangle. Gently crease the fold, being careful to keep the edges evenly aligned in the center and across the bottom.

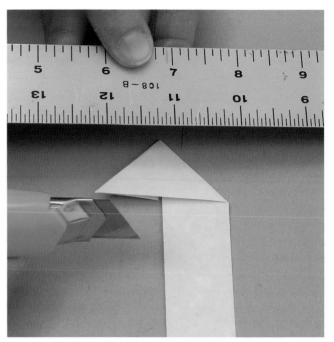

4. Turn the strip of paper over so that you can see where you will make your cut along the edge of the triangle.

5. Place your ruler so that the triangle is under it and the bottom is aligned with the edge, and cut along the ruler with your utility knife.

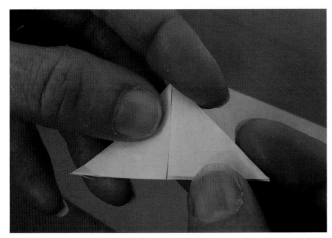

This should leave you with a single corner.

6. Trim a small piece of Filmoplast or other acid-free tape . . .

. . . and place it across the center of the triangle to hold the corner together. Make sure there is no gap in the middle between the edges, because you do not want the Filmoplast to stick to the artwork.

7. Use a small burnishing tool to smooth the Filmoplast into place. Repeat this process for each corner you wish to make.

8. The corners should slide easily onto the artwork you wish to mount.

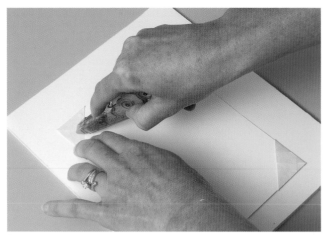

9. Place the piece facedown onto a clean surface and apply a small amount of double-sided tape to the back of each corner, being careful not to let the tape come into contact with the back of the artwork.

10. Turn the piece over and align it correctly on your mountboard.

11. Hold the piece in place while you press down on each corner with your thumb. Rub gently to smooth the corners into place.

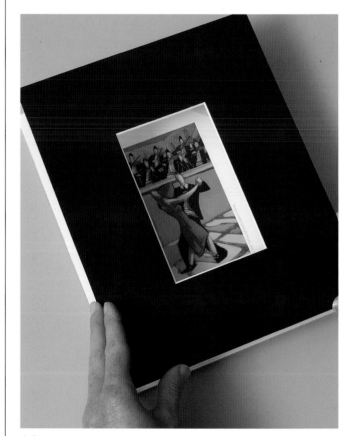

12. Place the matboard over the piece to be sure the corners are not visible at the edges of the mat. If they are, carefully trim them away with scissors.

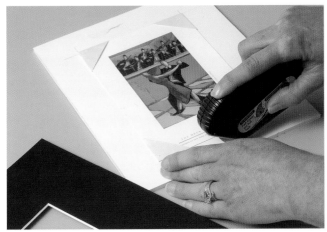

13. Apply double-sided adhesive to the mountboard on each side of the border and place your mat on top, being careful to align the edges.

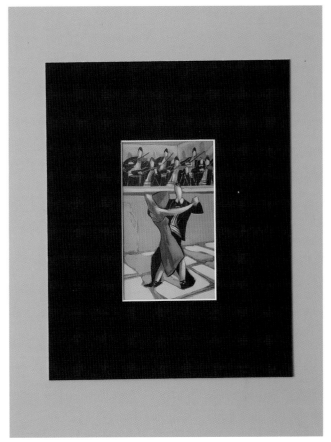

15. You now have a finished piece that is ready for framing.

14. Pound the matboard gently with a closed fist to press it into place.

An effective way to mount paper artwork that doesn't require conservation-quality mounting, such as a poster, is with a spray adhesive. Widely available in most art supply stores, spray adhesives allow you to coat the entire back of a piece, which gives a better hold and is therefore likely to endure. This technique is not reversible and is not a good choice for mounting valuable items of any kind. It is usually used on larger items, although it is quick and easy for small pieces, too.

Prepare your mountboard as described earlier. It is particularly important to have the outline clearly marked when using spray adhesives, since the back of the piece will be coated with a sticky layer when you place it onto the mountboard. Some sprays allow for repositioning, which means you can lift the artwork and replace it if you miss your mark, but it's best if you can get it properly placed the first time.

Because of the fumes involved, it is advisable to wear a safety mask and work outdoors or in a well-ventilated area. Avoid inhaling the fumes and keep in mind the highly flammable nature of spray adhesives. You will be spraying past the edges of the artwork, so be sure you are using some sort of dropcloth or backing, and be sure it is clean before you place your artwork down on it. A large piece of cardboard works well and is nicely disposable.

2. Position the can about 8 to 10 inches from the surface of the piece and spray the entire back of the art with an even motion.

1. Shake the can well before using it.

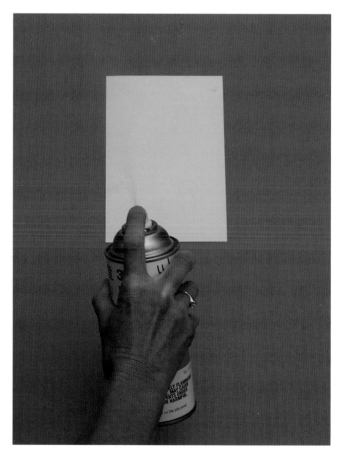

You want to evenly coat the entire surface. It is best to keep your arm moving back and forth both vertically and horizontally over the piece. This is the best way to give an even coating of adhesive without soaking any one section or entirely missing others. Be careful not to spray too heavily, or the adhesive may ooze out from under the work when it is placed, possibly marring the piece.

3. Holding the artwork carefully by the edges, place it faceup onto the mountboard.

4. If the piece is small, you can simply use your hand to smooth over the surface. (Make sure your hand is clean and free of adhesive residue.) If the piece is larger, you might want to use a handheld roller or burnisher to flatten out the work and eliminate air bubbles or wrinkles that might be trapped in the surface. Start at the center of the piece and work with side-to-side and up-and-down motions, continuing until the surface is smooth.

5. At this point it is a good idea to allow the adhesive time to dry and set. You can gently weight the surface with whatever materials you have at hand, if you wish. This is a good idea if the piece you are mounting is a poster or large piece that was rolled up and might not remain flat while the adhesive dries. Books work well as weights, as do bags of dried beans. Just be sure to protect the surface of the artwork before placing your weights atop it. Tissue paper, plastic wrap, or plexiglass are all acceptable to use.

6. When the adhesive has had a chance to dry, you are ready to attach the mat. Place strips of double-sided tape on the mountboard around the work.

7. Place the mat down over the piece and gently pound with your fist to help seal it in place.

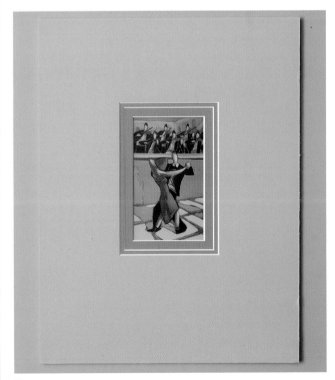

8. The piece is now ready for framing.

Mounting and framing needlework is a fairly basic process, although it does require some special techniques in order to anchor the work neatly and evenly in place within the frame. Most needlework is done on a special type of cloth called Aida, which is woven in neatly spaced rows, making it easy to keep your work lined up. Needlework done on linen or other, finer cloths may require a bit more work to find the rows. Before you begin, make sure your needlework is clean, and if it can be pressed, you might wish to iron it first with a warm iron and a protective cloth so that you have a nice, flat piece to work with. Be sure your hands are clean when handling the piece, because oils and dirt from your hands can smudge the fabric and the thread.

1. First, measure the size of the needlework. Do this by measuring from the uppermost stitch to the lowest stitch, and then across the width of the piece. Keep the tape measure straight across the work by lining it up with one of the rows in the cloth.

2. The measurements you come up with will be your image's dimensions. To this you will add a small border to allow the pattern to be fully visible within the mat. For this example, we added $5/8$ inch to each side. This is the size you will use to cut out your foam board.

Mounting

3. If you plan to mat your needlework project, you will need to cut a piece of foam board to match the outer dimensions of the mat and frame. You will then cut a smaller window from the foam board that will form the support for the needlework project itself. If you just wrapped the needlework around a small piece of foam board and then placed a mat around that, you would not be able to frame it neatly because the thickness of the foam board and the thickness of the surrounding mat would not match. Likewise, if you cut a large piece of foam board and used a separate piece for supporting the needlework, you would have a double thickness of foam board in the center, which would cause a bulge in the matting and wouldn't fit behind the frame glass. (If you do not plan to mat the work, you can simply cut a piece of foam board to fit it.)

Figure out your borders as outlined in the matting section, and cut the outer dimensions of the foam board to size using a ruler and utility knife. Foam board is generally too thick to cut with a mat cutter, so the utility knife is a better choice. Then mark the cut for the inner window as you would for cutting a mat, matching the dimensions of the image size and again using the utility knife and straight edge to get an even cut. Once you have the mountboard cut to size, check your measurements by laying the smaller piece of mountboard down and setting the needlework in place on top of it. Use your tape measure to be sure the size is right and the borders are even.

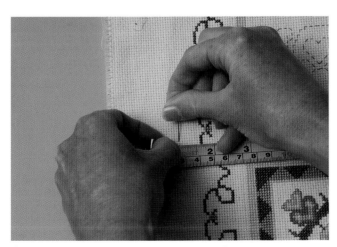

4. Using the tape measure, measure ⅝ inch from the edge of the needlework and place a small straight pin in the cloth. It doesn't matter where you start, since you will continue around the piece, measuring ⅝ inch from the edge of the pattern and placing straight pins into the cloth.

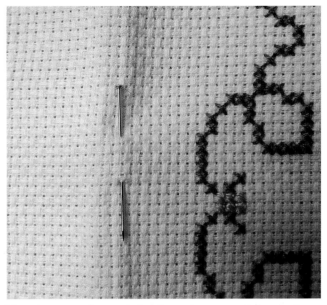

The pins must be straight along the rows of the cloth and should be pinned under three or four stitches.

5. When you are finished, the border of the work should be clearly marked with evenly spaced pins. The pins will make it easier to properly line up the piece around the mountboard.

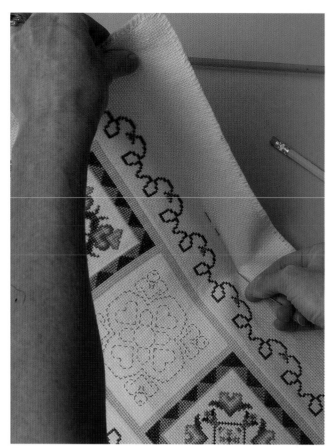

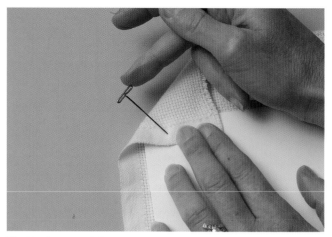

6. Check your measurements again to verify that the pins are properly placed, and gently score the border with a pin, holding the cloth at one end and dragging a pin or the eye end of a medium-size sewing needle along the edge to put a crease in the material. This will make it easier to fold around your mountboard.

8. Tuck one of the corners down over the foam board and secure it in place with a large pin. The pin does not have to go all the way through the cloth and mountboard; it simply has to tack the corner in place.

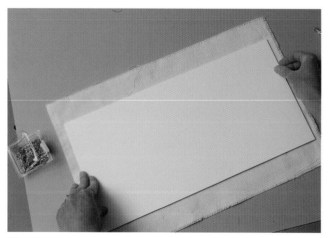

9. Turn the work and repeat with the other three corners, pinning them in folds down over the corners of the foam board.

7. Make sure your work surface is clean and lay the needlework facedown on it. Place your foam board down over the needlework and align the edges with the pins in the cloth.

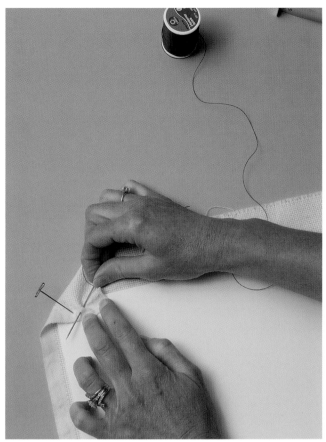

10. Thread a large needle with some sturdy thread. Upholstery thread works well, but cotton sewing thread will not be strong enough to hold the work together.

11. Start by sewing opposite corners together across the back of the work. Make a stitch in one corner close to the edge, then in the corner diagonally opposite, then in the first corner near the original stitch.

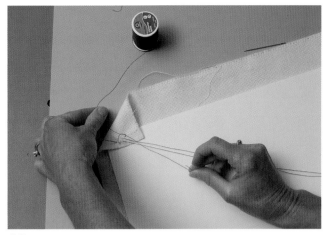

12. Tie off the thread by joining the two ends in a knot.

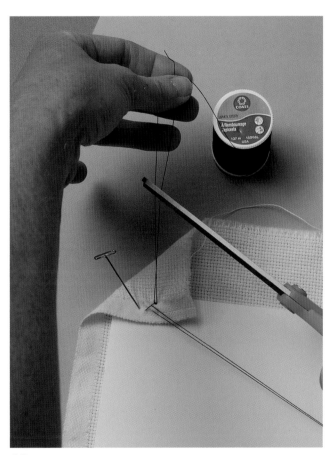

13. Clip the knot with scissors, leaving a fairly long thread.

Mounting

14. Do the same with the other two corners.

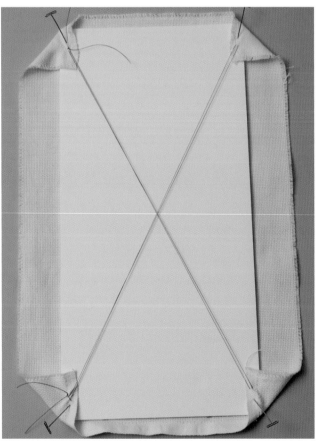

15. When you have finished, you will have an X across the back of the needlework, holding the corners in place.

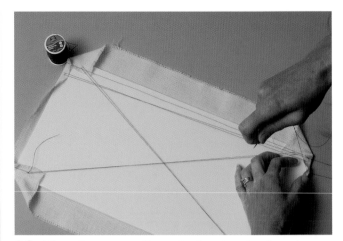

16. Thread your needle again, leaving the thread attached to the spool.

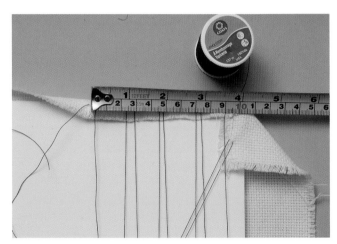

17. Sew the opposite sides of the work together by making small stitches about an inch apart across the back of the work. Keep gently pulling the thread off the spool so that you work with one continuous piece of thread.

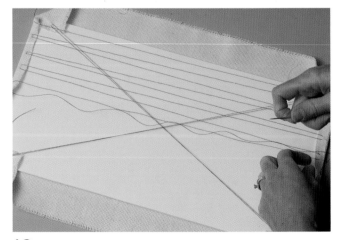

18. The needle should pass under two to four rows with each stitch. If you don't grab enough cloth with the stitch, it might weaken or tear, and if you take large stitches, the material might pucker when you pull it tight.

19. Make sure you are keeping the cloth in place along the mountboard by checking your pinned borders as you go and adjusting as necessary to keep the work straight. If the thread gets too tight, use your free hand to pull more off the spool and through the stitches, so that you have enough to work with as you proceed along the side of the work.

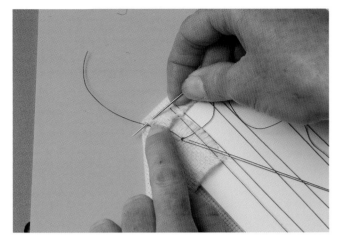

20. When you reach the opposite side from where you started sewing, pull the thread tight and make a final stitch in the corner flap of cloth to secure the thread.

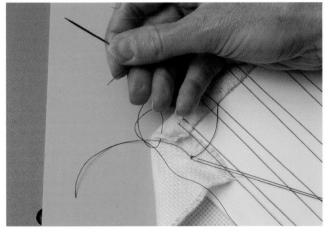

21. Tie a knot around the piece of thread that forms the X holding the corners in place.

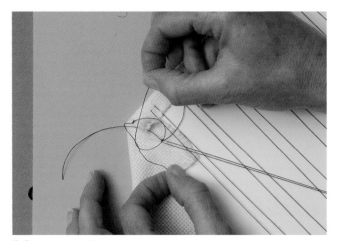

22. Pull the knot tight.

23. Clip the thread from the spool and secure that end in the same manner—tied around the thread forming the X. You should have a nice, even crosshatch of stitches across the long side of the work.

24. Put on clean rubber gloves. These will help you keep a grip on the cloth without worrying about fingerprints getting on the work as you are handling it.

25. Gently manipulate the cloth so that the edge of the mountboard is even along a single row of the cloth all the way along each of the sewn sides.

Use the pins you placed earlier as guidelines; they should line up at the edge of the cloth and mountboard. If they do not, check your measurements; you may need to tighten the thread at the back. You can do this by going over the sewn portion and pulling each stitch a little tighter. When you reach the other side, snip the extra thread off and re-tie the knot. When one side is done to your satisfaction, repeat the process for the other side.

26. Leaving the thread on the spool, secure it at one corner before proceeding down the short side to the opposite end and back up again.

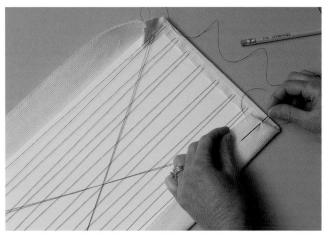

27. This will leave a neat crosshatch on the back of the work, perpendicular to the sewing you've already done. Sew the corner flaps down when you come to them by folding them neatly and putting your first and last stitch on the outer edge of the fold.

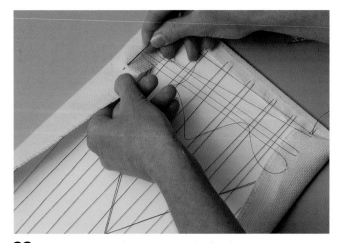

28. Continue stitching across the back.

56

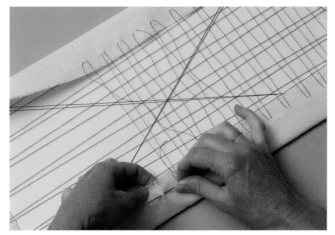

You will need to pull the thread through the cloth as you go.

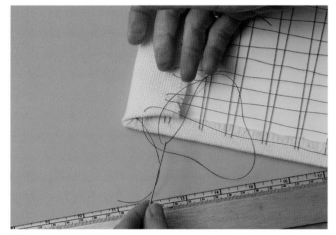

29. When you have secured the last corner and completed stitching the side, clip and knot the thread by looping it around the anchoring X.

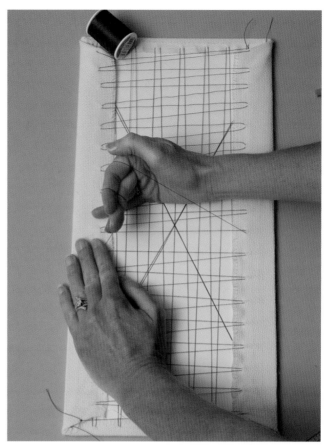

30. Then begin to work backward from the last stitch to the first to remove any slack in your thread.

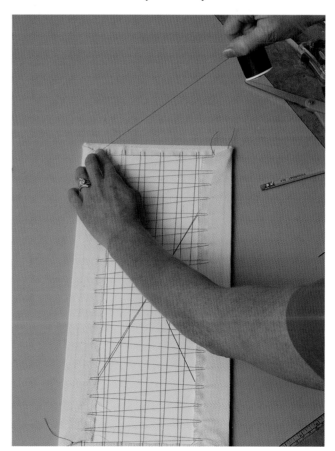

Gently pull the thread tight as you go.

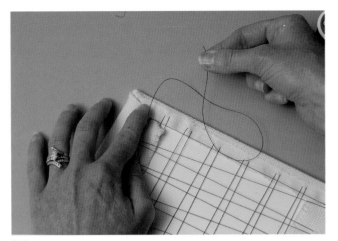

31. Clip and knot the corner close to the spool.

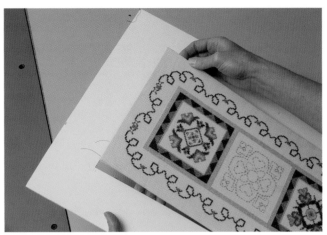

34. You are now ready to add the mat and frame of your choice.

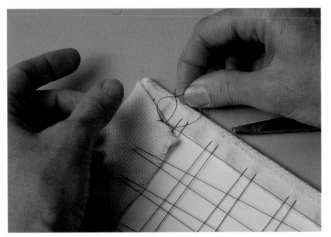

32. The completed work will have a neat network of criss-crossing threads with the large X holding the corners in place. Using your rubber gloves, even up the edges to follow a single row of the cloth, checking your measurements as you go.

33. Once the work is secured to your liking, if you plan to mat it, place it into the larger piece of foam board you prepared earlier. Press gently along the edges to make sure you have it flat within the mountboard.

4

Framing and Finishing

Selecting a Frame

Like matboard, frames come in a wide variety of colors, textures, and styles. You can buy ready-made frames in all sizes and colors, from simple, unpainted wooden frames to elaborate gold-leaf creations that are nearly works of art themselves. There are various frame textures that can bring out interesting patterns within an image. As in matting, there are no hard-and-fast rules for what type of frame goes best with what type of work, but different frames can give very different appearances to a piece of art.

Unpainted wooden frames are nice and simple, making for clean lines.

Metal frames come in a variety of shades and sometimes give a sleeker, more functional appearance.

Painted wood frames can bring out the colors and tones within a photo or other image. A frame painted to have some texture can add a more formal touch to a work and bring out colors within the mat or the image.

Bolder, more ornate frames can also add interesting touches to your work, although most are purchased ready-made and can't be assembled.

Painting courtesy Deljou Art Group

Don't be afraid to experiment with frames of various widths, materials, colors, and finishes. If you are buying a ready-made frame and can take the piece you have in mind with you, do so. Try several different styles of frame with it, keeping in mind how you plan to mat the work, the colors you wish to bring out or tone down, and the surroundings in which the frame will be displayed. Look at framed works in galleries, shops, homes, and businesses you visit, noting what you like and what you don't, and use that knowledge to choose your own frames. It is a matter of exploring what appeals to you and what fits your needs. There really is no wrong way to do it.

Metal frame kits are available in art supply stores and wherever else framing materials are sold. Each kit holds two identical lengths of metal as well as the hardware necessary for putting them together. In order to build a frame that is 8 x 10 inches, you would need to buy two kits: one 8-inch kit and one 10-inch kit. The wide variety of lengths available—from 3 inches all the way up to 30 inches—makes it easy to customize the measurements of the frame you wish to build, although the larger kits can be rather expensive. You can choose from silver- or gold-colored metal, as well as black. Metal frames have a sleek, modern look that works well with black and white photos and color abstract prints in particular.

Assembling the Frame

You will need a screwdriver in order to assemble the metal frame kit, but the other hardware (backing plates and spring clips) should be included. If it is not, you will need to purchase it separately, but it shouldn't cost more than a few dollars to gather everything you need.

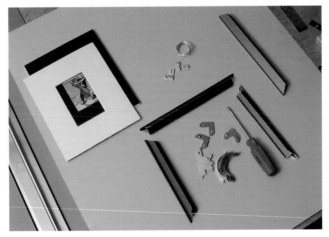

1. Lay your frame pieces out on your work surface as you will assemble them, with matching lengths opposite one another. This will help you to avoid putting two corners together only to discover you have joined the two 10-inch sides together instead of one side of each length.

2. There are two types of corner-shaped backing plates: plain ones and those with screws affixed at either end. They are usually marked, the plain ones with an A and the others with a B.

Pick up one of each and place the plain backing plate behind the other one. Align the edges.

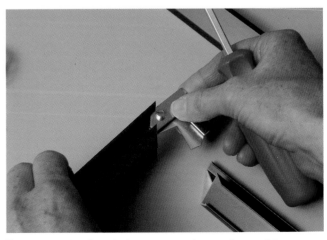

3. The back of each frame piece has a channel into which you can slide the paired plates.

Push the plates all the way into one of the sides until you can't move them any farther forward.

4. Now pick up another piece of the frame—be sure it is the correct length—and slide it onto the other side of the backing plates, moving it up until the edges of the frame pieces meet to form a corner.

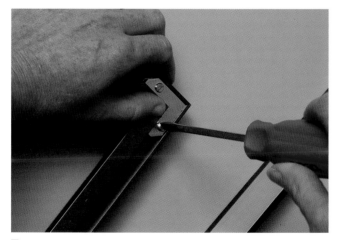

5. Tighten the screws on the backing plates to hold the pieces in place.

6. Turn the frame over and check the seam at the corner. It should be even. If it is not, adjust the tightness of the screws at the back until you have a nice, tight corner.

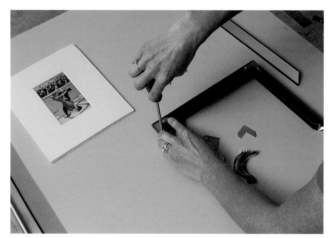

7. It is easiest to slide the artwork and mat in at the longer side of the frame, so it's best to attach the second short side of the frame at this point. At the other end of the longer side of your partially assembled frame, slide another pair of backing plates into the channel and place the second short side of the frame on them. Tighten the screws and check to make sure your corner is nice and even. You now have three completed sides. It is time to place your matted artwork into the frame before closing up the final side.

8. Place a towel down across your work surface. This will cushion the glass.

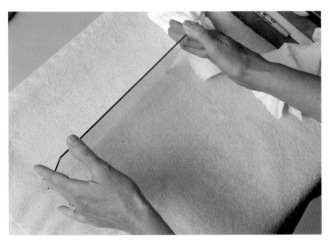

9. You'll need a piece of glass the size of the frame. Clean it thoroughly with glass cleaner and a cloth or paper towel before placing it into the frame.

Any dust or dirt left on the glass will show up in the final product and detract from the overall effect, so be sure to wipe away all traces of lint, dust, or dirt and to get fingerprints and other smudges off as well.

Handling Glass

Always handle glass carefully with your fingers flat across the edges or with a cloth between your fingers and the edge. Do not try to pinch the glass with your fingertips or grip it tightly. The edges of the glass remain sharp and can cut you if you handle it carelessly.

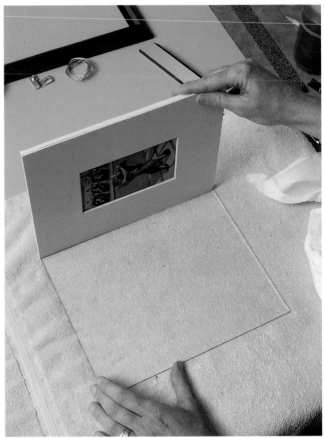

10. Lay the clean piece of glass down on the towel and place your matted artwork vertically alongside it. Make sure the mat is free of dust, lint, and smudges as well, or they will show up under the glass. If the mat is smudged, you can usually rub the area clean with a soft eraser or clean cloth, using gentle motions. (Be sure your eraser is clean before you begin, or you can further smudge a light-colored mat.)

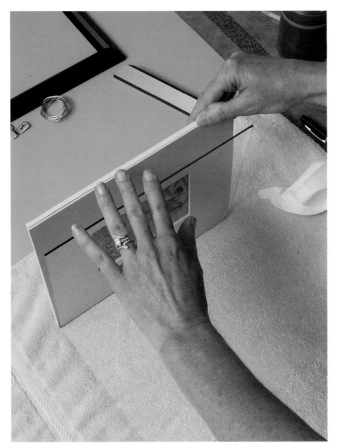

11. Align the matted artwork with the edge of the glass and lift the glass carefully off the towel, sandwiching the two together.

12. Make sure the glass and the mat are a proper fit.

Note: Some frame kits come with hanging hardware that must be put in place *before* the final leg of the frame is attached. Check your hanging clips to see if you need to attach them at this point or not.

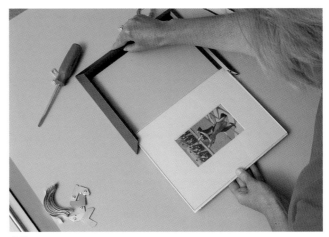

13. Lay the three-sided metal frame faceup on your work surface. Slide the glass and the matted artwork together into the frame. Lift the open end of the frame up to be sure the glass is all the way in, then turn the frame over to attach the remaining side.

14. Place the two remaining pairs of plates together and slide them onto either end of the remaining frame piece.

15. Slide the remaining piece onto the rest of the frame. This part can be a bit tricky; it is best to try to slide both ends evenly at the same time.

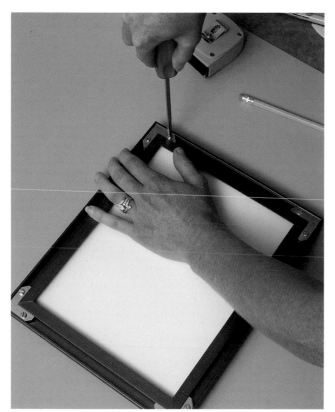

16. Hold the frame together and screw down the backing plates on each side until they fit snugly.

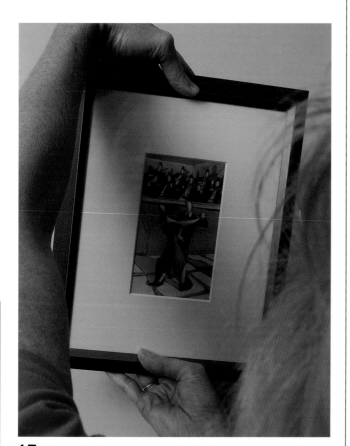

17. Turn the frame over and check your corners. Do this carefully, because you have not fully secured the artwork yet, and it might still be a bit loose.

18. Examine the front of the work for smudges or dirt you might have missed before. You might need to take the frame apart and clean the mat if you did miss something. If you are satisfied with the way it looks, turn the frame over carefully and lay it down on your work surface.

19. Springclips are then inserted between the back of the frame and the mountboard to hold the artwork firmly in place, making it safe to handle and hang the frame. Place the clip down so that the curve faces up, and press down with your thumb on the middle of the curve.

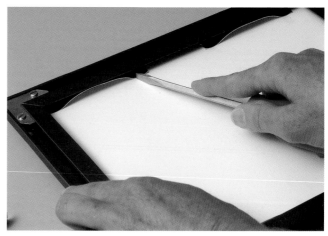

20. Holding the clip pressed down, slide it under the edge of the frame. You can use a screwdriver to gently push the clip into place. Repeat this process for each side. Use enough clips so that they are evenly and fairly closely spaced. Here we used one clip on each short side and two on the longer sides of an 8 x 10-inch frame.

Attaching Hardware and Wire

Metal frames have channeled backs that allow the use of specialized hanging hardware that may or may not come with them. Check the packaging when purchasing your frame kit to see it if includes these clips, particularly if you wish to hang the frame on a wall. If they do not come with the kit, they are usually available for purchase wherever you buy the kit. You will also need wire with which to hang the frame, and that will most likely not be included with your kit.

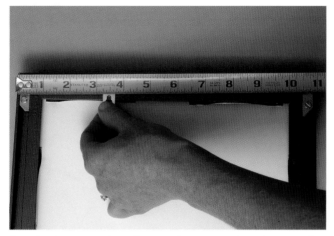

1. The hanging clips fit into the channel at the top of the frame and slide freely along it until you tighten the screw, allowing you to choose the placement for each side. It is best to place the clips about a third of the way down each vertical side of the frame. This will place the wire across the back of the work at a point where the frame will be well-balanced and stable.

2. When you have determined where you want the clips to be, simply tighten them on with the screwdriver.

3. Cut a length of wire that extends beyond the edges of the frame by about 3 or 4 inches on either side.

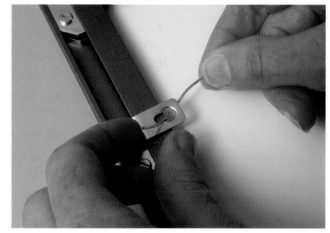

4. Thread it through the openings in the hanging hardware on both sides of the frame by going down through the holes.

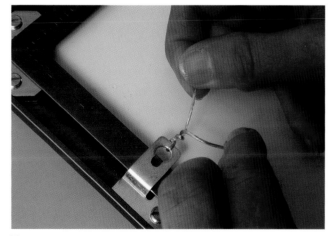

5. Knot the wire on one side and then wrap it around itself several times.

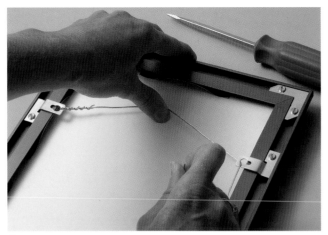

6. Do the same on the other side.

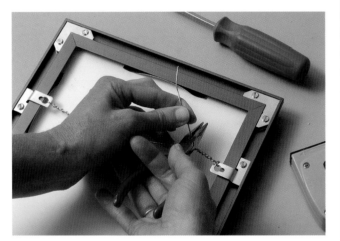

7. You can trim away any excess wire once you have wrapped it well.

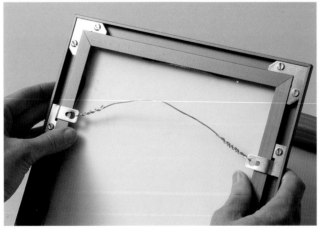

8. You now have a metal frame that is ready for hanging and display.

Like metal frames, wooden frames are available in kits containing two equal-length sides and connecting hardware. You have to buy two kits of different sizes to make the frame you need. The frames are designed with notches at the back of each corner into which you insert small pegs to hold the frame together. You will need wood glue and a clean cloth to complete the assembly. For this frame, we used small nails to anchor the art into place and double-sided tape to secure the backing.

Assembling the Frame

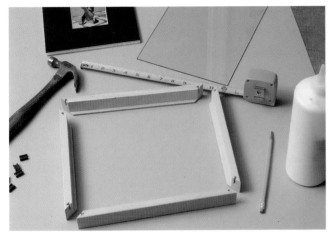

1. Lay out the frame as you want it to look when finished, with sides of equal length opposite one another.

2. Select a frame piece and apply wood glue evenly to the surface of one corner. Use a moderate amount of glue—too much and the joint will not fit together tightly enough; too little and the frame will not hold. The entire surface of the corner should be evenly coated with the glue, but don't fill the notch with it.

3. Place the glued corner against the unglued corner of the proper side and press them together, lining up the notches so that they form a hole for the peg.

4. Place a peg into the hole and gently tap it into place with a hammer. The peg should fit all the way down into the hole so there is nothing protruding past the plane of the frame.

Framing and Finishing

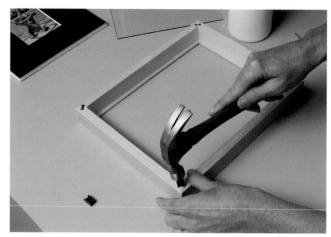

5. Check all sides of the joint and wipe away any glue that has seeped out. It is important to get all traces of the glue wiped away before it dries. Glue on the front of the frame will look messy, while glue on the inside edge of the lip can interfere with the fit of the glass against the frame.

Be sure to wipe away excess glue as you go so it doesn't dry or get gummy on your frame.

7. Allow the glue to dry for a few hours. You don't need to set the frame in a vise if you can leave it flat and undisturbed on your work surface. Once the glue is dry and set, you are ready to put your project together.

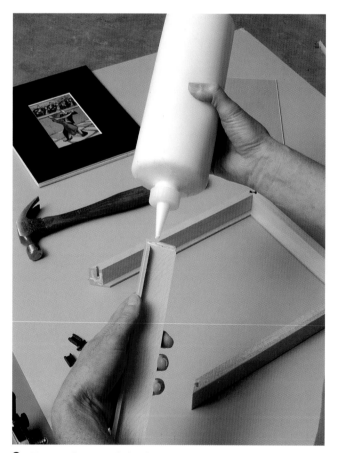

6. Proceed around the frame, putting glue on one side of each corner, aligning the corners so the notches come together, and tapping the pegs into place at each corner. Unlike the metal frame, where you must inset the matted artwork before closing up the frame, with the wooden frame kits you build the entire frame and then insert the artwork from the back.

Framing the Art

1. Clean your glass carefully and sandwich it with the clean, matted artwork (see page 64–65). Lay them faceup on your work surface, and place the frame down over it.

2. Carefully pick up the frame and its contents . . .

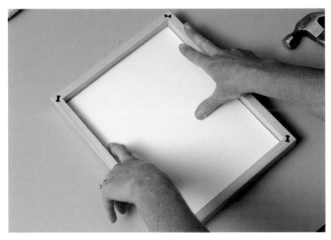

. . . and turn it over, placing it facedown onto your work surface. Run your finger around the inside edge of the frame to be sure the glass, mat, and mountboard are gently pressed into the front of the frame.

3. To hold the framed materials in place, you need to drive several small nails into the edge of the frame all the way around. Place one nail every few inches and tap it gently into place with a hammer.

You want to drive the nails in far enough that they are anchored in the frame, but not so far that they come out the other side or don't hold the artwork in place. Leave about an inch of each nail above the frame. Don't pound too hard or you could break the frame or damage the glass. If a claw or ball-peen hammer seems too big, try a smaller tack hammer. You need to pay special attention to securing the corners, driving nails in close to each one.

Framing and Finishing

When you are finished, you should have an even row of nails all around the back of the frame.

4. You can also use glazing points to secure the framed materials in place.

The advantage of using glazing points is that you needn't use a hammer. You can simply push them into the wood with a screwdriver.

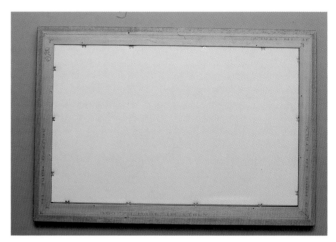

5. Space them much the same as you would the nails.

6. Brad guns, also called point drivers, are also available and are useful if you plan to do a lot of framing.

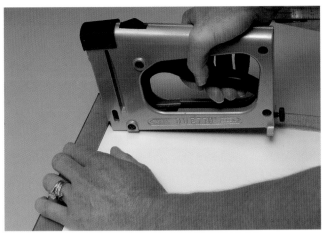

To use a brad gun, you place the edge against the inside of the frame and pull the handle, driving the glazing point into place.

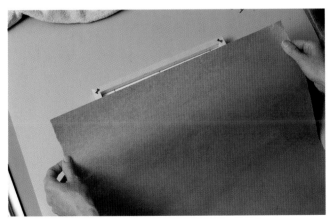

7. No matter how secure the artwork is in the frame, the next step is to apply double-sided tape around the outer edge of the back of the frame.

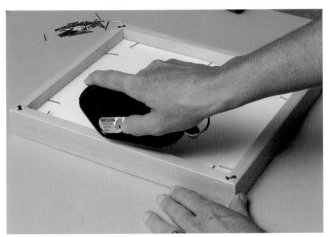

8. Lay a piece of acid-free backing paper over the frame. The paper should be large enough to cover the entire frame with a few extra inches of paper on each side. You can leave it attached to the roll while you lay it over the frame, or you can trim it off the roll before doing so.

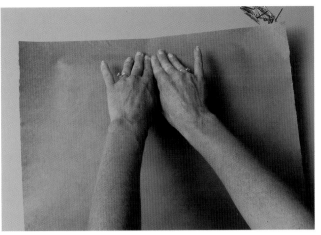

9. When you have laid the paper in place over the back of the frame, use your fingers to smooth the paper so it fits nicely across the back.

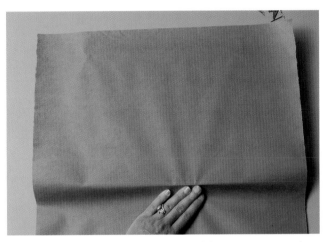

It shouldn't be so loose that it wrinkles or sags into the frame.

10. Use your fingers to pinch a crease along the outer edge of the frame, pushing the paper down along the side and pressing it against the adhesive at the same time.

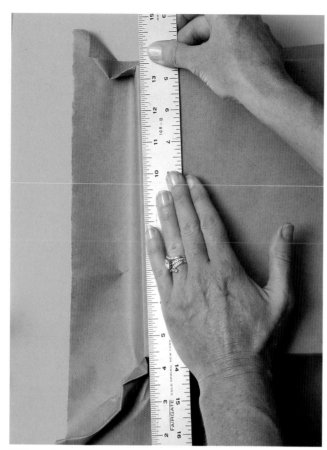

11. Take your straight edge and place it along a side of the frame.

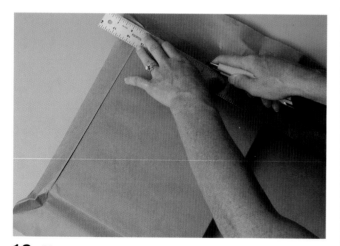

12. Use your utility knife to cut the paper, holding it between the edge of the ruler and the edge of the frame. Press firmly on the straight edge, but don't press too hard on the utility knife, or you might scar the frame. If your blade is sharp, it should cut the paper easily without too much pressure being applied.

13. Repeat for each side, then remove the excess paper.

You should be left with a small border of frame around the back so that the paper will not be visible when the work is turned around.

Attaching Hanging Hardware

SCREW EYES

The hardware that secures the frame to the hanging wire looks like a screw with a loop at the top instead of a flat head. It is screwed into the back of the frame and the wire is attached through its eye.

1. The screw eyes should be placed about a third of the way down the vertical sides of the frame. Use a tape measure to get an accurate placement, and make a small hole in the wood using an awl. You can use a drill if you have one, but an awl works well with the soft wood and there is less risk that you will make too deep a hole. Push the awl in about $^1/_4$ inch, less if you are using smaller screws.

2. Screw the eyelets into the holes as far as they will go.

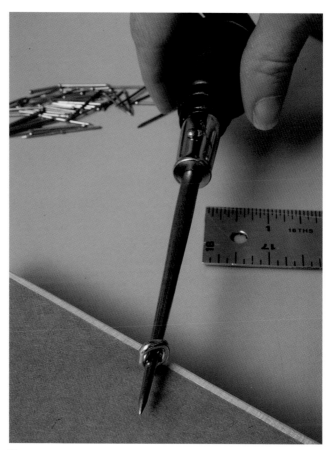

3. You can use the awl to tighten the final few twists of the screw. Leave the eye aligned vertically with the edge of the frame.

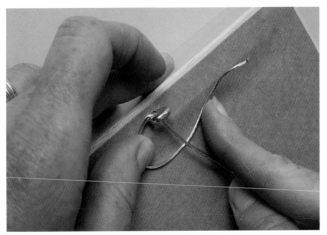

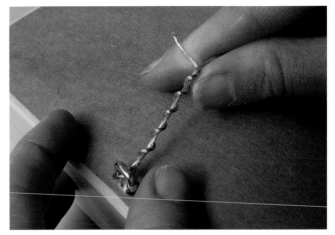

4. Cut a piece of hanging wire about 6 inches wider than the width of your frame. You can simply lay the wire across the back and leave a few inches on either side and snip it off the spool. Insert the wire into the eye of one of the screws from the inner side toward the outer side. Loop it around under the longer length of wire . . .

5. Wrap the end several times around the longer piece and snip it off.

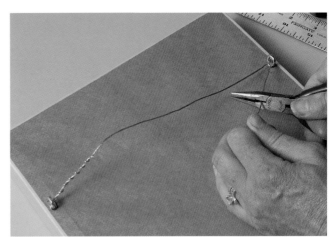

. . . and pass it through the eye again, this time going in the opposite direction, from the outside to the inside edge. Pass the end of wire under the loop you just made and pull it tight.

6. Repeat this process for the other side of the frame. Your work is now ready for display.

SAWTOOTH HANGERS

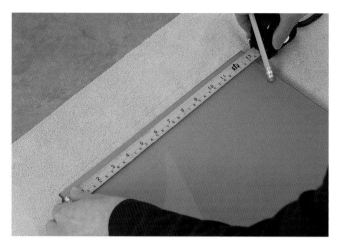

1. To attach a sawtooth hanger to your frame, measure the width of the frame across the back and find your center point. Here the frame is 13 inches wide, so the center point is $6^{1}/_{2}$ inches.

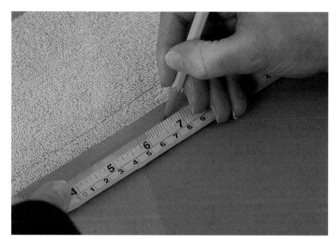

2. Mark the center point with a pencil and align the center dot on the sawtooth hanger over that mark.

3. Using a hammer, gently affix the hanger to the frame. Some sawtooth hangers can be embedded directly into the frame . . .

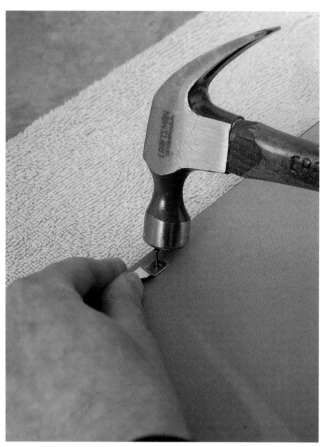

. . . while others require the use of two small nails or brads to hold them in place.

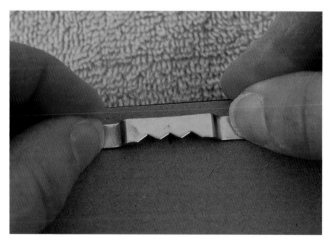

4. Be very careful when pounding in the hanger so that you don't break the glass or otherwise damage the piece.

LARGE OR HEAVY PIECES

Large or heavy framed works often require more than simple hanging hardware and wire strung across the back. Some items should not be hung with wire at all—for instance, wire can mar the back surface of the mirror, resulting in an imperfect reflection. For projects such as these, you can purchase special hardware for hanging them that will eliminate the need to string wire and that will provide support for the weight of the framed piece.

2. Place a screw in each hole (there are usually two per hanger) and fasten the hanger into place.

1. You want to attach the mirror hangers about $1/3$ of the way down from the top edge of the frame. This distance provides the most stability.

Measure each side, and lay the hangers at the proper position before you screw them in to be sure you have even placement across the piece. If you place them unevenly, the piece will look crooked when hung on the fixtures. You can use an awl to poke a small hole through the hangers into the frame, or you can simply use a drill.

The finished frame, shown here with fasteners (see page 90).

Choosing the Wood

The first step in making a picture frame is to choose your wood. Wood for picture frames can come from a variety of sources. One of the best and easiest to find is molding used in home-building projects, such as cabinetry or door moldings. These are readily available in most home-improvement stores and lumberyards, and you can even buy them pre-finished and pre-painted, making it extremely easy to build a simple frame. You can buy packages of molding pre-cut to specific sizes, or you can purchase a longer length of routed molding and trim it yourself. Whatever you choose, make sure the molding has a groove wide enough to hold the glass and your matted artwork.

Apart from molding, you can also simply use boards planed to the desired thickness and cut to size. Or you can use "found" wood—wood recycled from other projects, such as old barn doors, to make rustic-looking frames.

When choosing the wood for your frame, you should consider elements such as the natural shade of the wood, its durability and weight (for hanging purposes), and whether or not the finished frame is going to be stained, finished, or painted. Softer, lighter-weight woods are easier to work with and hang. The heavier woods tend to be more durable and less prone to damage. Check out a variety of woods and see what you like and what suits your needs.

Some examples of pre-finished and pre-painted molding.

Staining and Painting

The decision to stain or paint your frame is an individual one. A stained frame can bring interesting details in the artwork into more vivid detail; a painted one can be a bridge between the image displayed and the décor of the room it will be in. Both techniques can complement the mat color, making the piece more pleasing to the eye. Leaving the wood as it is and simply finishing it to bring out the natural warmth of the grain is also a possibility.

Since it is simpler to get a uniform shade when dealing with one large piece than with four smaller pieces, it is best to stain or paint the framing materials before cutting them apart. Any distortions in color that appear at the corners after cutting can be hidden with touch-up work.

To stain the frame, have the molding ready, along with a soft paintbrush and a small amount of the stain you have chosen. The size of the frame will determine the size of your brush, but generally, a smaller brush is more easily guided along narrow molding.

First, lightly and gently sand the molding. Then apply the stain in a smooth motion that follows the grain of the wood. Be sure to cover all the wood evenly and uniformly or you will get light and dark patches in the finished frame. Use the brush to smooth over any drips or streaks until you have a uniformly coated piece of wood. Remember to stain the inner and outer edges, since they will also be visible in the finished frame. Prop the molding faceup a few inches above your work surface. You can place it on small blocks of wood or something similar that will allow it to dry with nothing touching the newly stained portion. It is best to let it dry overnight or for several hours. You then may wish to lightly sand it and apply another coat of stain if it does not seem dark enough to suit.

To paint a frame, use the same process as for staining your molding, but apply a coat of primer or base coat to help the paint adhere to the wood without streaking or leaving the finished product prone to peeling. Allow plenty of time for the paint to dry, and sand lightly between coats.

Once you are satisfied with the appearance of your molding, whether you are leaving the wood grain natural, staining it, or painting it, the final step is to apply a coat of sealer. This is best done after the frame has been assembled. Sealing the frame will work to protect your framed art from contact with resins in the wood of the frame itself and seal out moisture from the frame, which can damage both frame and art. Usually, two coats of an acrylic-polymer matte-finish sealer will do the job nicely. (High-gloss sealers tend to distract from the presentation of the artwork.) Apply the sealer with a brush that has been thoroughly cleaned and use a clean work surface.

There are a couple methods for applying the sealer and allowing it to dry. You can do three sides of the frame completely and clamp it into a vise along the side you haven't sealed, going back to seal that side after the rest has been allowed to dry. If you do this, use a soft cloth between your frame and the vise in order to protect the wood. You can also seal the front side of the frame, remembering to get the inner and outer edges, and prop the frame face up on a few blocks of wood to allow it to dry. When it has dried, simply turn it over, seal the back side, and allow it to dry as well.

Measuring

In order to know how much wood or molding to buy, you need to calculate the size of your frame and determine your measurements. The corners of a basic frame are cut at angles so they fit together. This means that in addition to adding up the dimensions of the height and width of the interior of the frame, you must add two times the width of the molding to each side of your frame in order to get your final sum. For example, for a 16 x 20-inch frame made with 2-inch molding, you need to add the lengths of the sides to get the inner dimensions (16 + 16 + 20 + 20 = 72 inches). To this figure, you must then add the extra inches you will need for each corner—for 2-inch molding, you will add 16 inches (2 x 8). This gives you a final length of 88 inches, which is how much molding you will need to purchase in order to make the frame.

For this project, we used pre-finished and pre-painted picture frame molding, which is available anywhere framing supplies are sold. Some places can even cut it to size for you if you lack the space to haul or store a long length of uncut molding.

Cutting to Size

If you are going to cut your own molding, you will need a miter saw to allow you to cut the proper angle into the corners. *Always* wear eye protection when operating a miter saw.

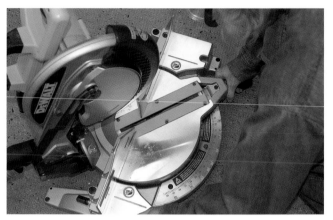

1. It is easiest to cut one end of the molding first so you can use the corner of the inner angle when measuring out the first piece of your frame.

2. Set the miter angle for 45 degrees and place the wood facedown so that you can trim off the end.

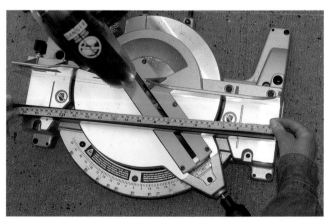

3. Starting at the inside corner of the angle, measure 16 inches from that point and make a pencil mark along the top edge of the molding.

The mark must be visible while you are cutting, so make sure it is large enough to read easily.

4. In order to get the opposite sides of the frame properly cut, with both angles facing the proper way, you will need to reset the saw for 45 degrees in the opposite direction.

5. Place the molding facedown along the guide and cut at your 16-inch mark.

6. You can now use this cut piece to mark off a similar length on the remaining molding. Simply match up the edges of the angle with the angled end of the longer piece of molding (or some other separate piece, if you had them cut to smaller lengths) and make a pencil mark across the molding along the end of the 16-inch piece.

7. Set the saw to the proper 45-degree angle and cut the molding. You now have both 16-inch pieces of your frame ready. Follow the same procedure to get your 20-inch pieces. Remember to double-check all your measurements *before* you cut the first piece, and check to be sure that the first piece you cut is the proper size before you use it to mark off the second piece. Take care to ensure that the corners are cut properly, with the inside corners on the same side so you can make four neat corners.

8. Test that the lengths of wood are the same size by placing them together and running your fingertip over each end.

There should be no difference in length detectable by touch.

Putting the Frame Together

1. When using stained or painted moldings, the cutting process reveals the plain wood interior. It can also create small nicks or chips in the edges of the molding. These defects are sometimes visible at the corners when the frame is put together and will diminish the effect of the finished frame if not corrected.

In order to eliminate them, use a touch-up marker that matches the color of the frame and draw a thick line around the front and bottom edges of each end of the molding.

These special pens are available in some craft and art supply shops and home-improvement supply stores. Don't use regular magic marker or other writing implements: they use ink, which gives a different look to the touched-up spots. Also, the ink may not be waterproof, and it could smear and discolor when glue is applied.

A corrected corner.

2. Put together one corner of the frame by setting the ends of a long side and a short side together as they will be when framed. Check that the corners match up well, and then arrange the pieces of molding so the back sides come together and the corner angles form one plane.

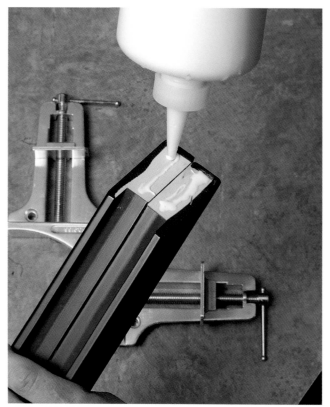

3. Apply a moderate amount of wood glue to both pieces. You don't have to coat the entire surface with glue. A good, even bead drawn with the tip of the bottle along each piece should be sufficient. If you use too much glue, it will keep the joint from meeting properly, and if you use too little, the frame is likely to break apart.

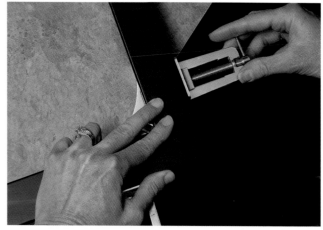

4. Join the edges and even them up by using your fingertips to feel the seam. It should feel even, with no misalignment on either side. Make sure the edges are even before proceeding or the frame will not be square. A small amount of glue will seep out along the edges and can be easily wiped clean with a rag or other cloth. Complete the other corners of the frame by repeating the same process, matching the angles and applying the glue.

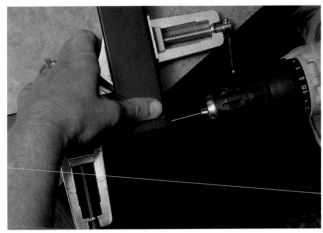

5. Use a drill with a small bit to make a hole near the edge of each corner. These are where you will place small nails that will strengthen the frame and help it to hold together better. It is best to offset them a bit, putting one nail close to the front of the frame and the other side close to the back of the frame so that they will not meet halfway through the frame. It is a good idea to use a clamp or a vise to hold your frame corner in order to drill the hole and drive the nail. Corner clamps, which can easily be attached to the side of your work surface or hold the frame without being attached to anything else, are available in hardware and home-building supply stores and will come in handy if you intend to make many frames.

6. Holding the frame corner together securely with the clamp, tap a small nail into the first hole.

7. When you have driven it down close to the edge of the frame, use a nail set to finish it. The nail set will spare the frame from being hit directly with the hammer, which could damage or skew it, and it will allow you to sink the nail all the way into the frame for a neater finish.

8. Do the same for the other side of the corner.

9. You will notice that there are small holes in the sides of the frame where you drove in your nails. You can fill these with wood putty. Be sure to choose a putty that matches the shade of the wood.

11. Wipe up any putty residue from the frame. It will harden when it dries and can mar the finish.

12. Allow time for the glue to dry overnight, if possible, or for at least 8 to 12 hours. It is not really necessary to clamp all four corners or keep the frame in a vise if you have nailed it together and are able to lay it flat and undisturbed to dry and set. Just make sure the corners are not under any stress during the process.

10. Use a putty knife to fill the holes . . .

. . . and smooth the frame surface so there are no defects in it.

If you wish to cut your own glass, you must first take some simple precautions. Remember to handle all glass carefully—even the flat edge has sharp corners that can cut you if you are careless. Cutting glass also produces glass "dust," which can cut or irritate your skin, your eyes, or any other part of you that comes into contact with it. Handle the glass as little as possible, clean up the site as soon as you are finished, and wear appropriate eye protection when cutting. You may also want to practice on a scrap piece of glass first, to get a feel for how hard to press, to get used to the sensation and sound of scoring the glass, and to learn how to break the glass accurately and safely.

Before you begin, determine your measurements. Standard frame-size measurements match glass size; for example, here we used an 11 x 14-inch frame, so we needed an 11 x 14-inch piece of glass. It is always best to check the measurement across the front of the frame to determine what size piece to cut, in case there are any small inaccuracies in the size. It is much easier to cut an 11 x 13$\frac{7}{8}$-inch piece of glass than to try to shave $\frac{1}{8}$ inch off a cut piece.

1. Lay towels over your work surface. Be sure you have an area large enough to protect the entire sheet of glass, and be sure the surface is flat and solid. Clean the glass thoroughly with glass cleaner and a clean rag or paper towel. You don't want any dirt on the surface that might interfere with scoring the glass.

2. Starting from one corner of the larger sheet, use a tape measure and a Sharpie or similar marker to mark your measurements, then use a straight edge to draw the borders of your final piece.

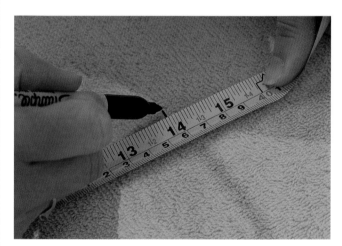

You can use a marker to draw directly on the glass since the very edges of the glass will be hidden behind the frame.

This approach yields more accurate results than drawing the lines on a piece of paper and laying the glass over it.

3. You will need to draw one of your lines completely across the glass. This is because you will need to cut the glass cleanly across one side before cutting the other edge. It is nearly impossible to cut partway along a piece of glass. It simply does not break properly that way.

4. You are now ready to use the glass cutter. You are not actually cutting down through the glass with the cutter; instead, you are putting a deep score mark into the surface of the glass. This weakens it along that line and makes it more likely to break at that point. However, it is still possible to break the glass improperly, so be very careful not to lean on the glass or place it on an unstable or uneven surface, or it could break prematurely or in the wrong place.

You first need to cut all the way across the sheet of glass. Hold the cutter in your hand as shown, with your thumb providing the pressure as you cut. Using a firm, even pressure, start at the outside edge and follow the line across the glass.

It is best to position the glass so that you are starting at the top and pulling the cutter down toward yourself, rather than trying to push it away from your body.

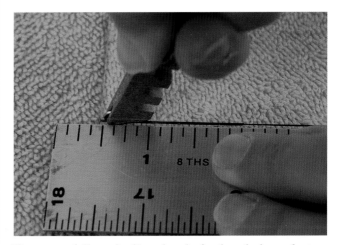

If you can follow the line cleanly freehand, do so, but using the straight edge is a good idea until you have had more practice. Place the head of the cutter against the side of the straight edge and pull it toward you, keeping an even pressure.

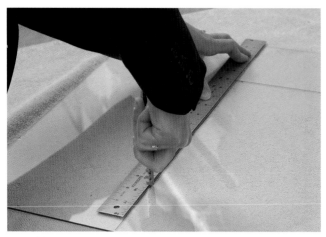

Cut all the way across along the line. You should be able to hear a slight grinding sound as the blade scores the glass.

5. When you have completed the cut, move the straight edge away and use the end of the handle of the cutter to tap gently all the way along the score mark. This helps to further weaken the glass along that line.

6. Use your thumbs to carefully press down along the line. Do not press on either side of the line, but directly on it, starting near the top, moving down a few inches, and pressing again.

The glass will snap along the line when it is sufficiently weakened by the pressing. It then may be cleanly lifted away.

8. As an alternative, you can carefully slide the glass to the edge of your work surface until the cut line is *exactly* aligned with the edge, then snap it with slight upward pressure on the unsupported side. Never press down on the outer piece of glass—you are much more likely to break it improperly or drop it when it snaps. This maneuver takes practice, and it is best to keep the piece you are cutting on the table, which may or may not be practical depending on the size of the sheet.

9. If the glass does not break properly, you will have to determine if you can rescore the line and try again or if you need to start over using another sheet of glass. Generally, if the piece you need to trim is not too small, it can be cut away with another pass from the cutter, but keep in mind the risks of handling smaller, unevenly broken shards of glass and take precautions accordingly.

10. Use a paper towel to remove any bits of glass produced by the scoring and carefully clean the glass again. You are now ready to place it into your frame.

Artist's canvases come in two types: unstretched and stretched. An unstretched canvas is simply a piece of canvas with no internal support structures. A stretched canvas contains an internal wooden frame over which the canvas has been pulled taut and fastened around the edges, either with staples or small nails, prior to painting. It has a slight depth due to the stretcher bars, which are usually $1/2$ to 1 inch thick.

An example of a stretched canvas.

Since most finished canvases you purchase will be stretched, this section deals with framing stretched canvasses only. If you do obtain a work of art on unstretched canvas, you will need to inquire of the artist or seller how best to display the work. Stretching the work after it is painted will ruin the piece, and depending on the medium and how it is used, conventional framing might also do damage.

Generally speaking, oil paintings are not covered with glass when framed. The texture of the paint sometimes does not allow for it, if it is thickly applied, and the glass also may lead to problems with moisture, which can become trapped and lead to damage. Glass can also obscure the pleasing textured appearance of the brushstrokes.

1. First, protect the painting and frame by covering your work surface with some clean towels. Make sure you cover a space larger than the area of the painting.

2. Make sure the frame is clean and lay it facedown on the work surface.

3. Set the canvas facedown in the frame, aligning it first along one edge (either the vertical or the horizontal), and then lowering it gently down so it fits into the frame.

Because a stretched canvas contains an internal frame already, it will probably be thicker than the frame and will protrude from the back.

4. The best way to fasten the canvas to the frame is to use fasteners that allow for the offset between the back of the frame and the back of the canvas. Nailing the canvas into the frame is possible but not recommended. Not only will you be unable to reverse the nailing without virtually destroying the frame, but you will also pierce the sides of the canvas, which can tear and suffer other damage. It is always best to allow for the reversal of your framing work without damage so you have the option of changing things in the future.

The fasteners need to be evenly spaced around the work and to provide adequate support for the weight of the painting and the frame. Lay them out before attaching them to be sure you are spacing them properly. They should be placed close to each corner and then evenly spaced along the longer side, if necessary. You want no more than about 12 inches between the hardware, and much less if the piece is very heavy. When you have the fasteners placed where you like them, use an awl or other sharp tool to poke a hole into the frame through the hole in the fastener. *Do not* punch a hole into the canvas stretcher bar. You don't ever want to puncture the canvas you are framing.

Then use a drill or screwdriver to insert a screw through the hole and secure the fastener to the frame. Again, it is best not to use nails. Be sure you are using a screw that is long enough to provide support but not so long that it will go through the front of the frame. Complete this process for each fastener.

Bump-Ons

To affix bump-ons, simply peel them one at a time off their adhesive backing and press them into place near the bottom corners of the work, where it is most likely to come into contact with the wall.

Here, we affixed them to the bottom edge of the canvas stretcher bars rather than to the frame itself because the thicker canvas is the part of the piece that will touch the wall first, not the corners of the frame.

Depending on the kind of attachment you placed on your frame, you will need to make one or two holes in your wall and affix some sort of hanging hardware. It is important to properly measure both the frame and the wall space in order to get the piece square and straight in the space you envision. You should measure vertically, either down from the ceiling or up from the floor or the back of a chair or couch over which the piece will hang. In this case, we measured from the back of a sofa upward to the proper point.

1. Start by taking a measurement from the top of the frame to the top of the hangers on each side. If you used wire, simply pull the wire taut and measure down the center of the back of the frame to the top edge of the wire. This determines the distance from the top of the frame to where the hanger will need to be. On this large piece, the hangers are $13^5/8$ inches down on each side. Be sure to measure for both sides when you use mirror hangers.

2. Now measure the width between hangers—*not* the width of the entire frame. Divide that measurement by 2 to get the center point of the piece. For example, here, the width between the hangers is 34 inches, which gives us a center point at 17 inches.

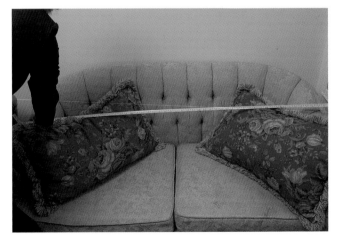

3. What you will eventually do is mark the center point on the wall in light pencil, then measure out from either side to get your fastener points.

You must now find the center point of the furniture. This sofa is 57 inches wide, placing the center point at $28^1/2$ inches.

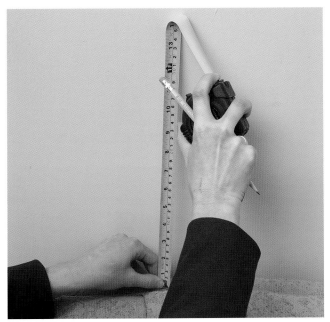

4. To find the horizontal placement, measure up from the top of the center of the sofa to wherever you want the bottom of the frame to be. This measurement is up to you, and is based on whatever looks most pleasing. Don't just pick a number; check the measurement along the wall to be sure the distance looks good to you. For this project, we used a distance of 10 inches.

5. Now measure the frame to determine the distance from the bottom edge to the tops of the hangers. Here, that distance is 33⅝ inches.

6. Again, if you are using two hangers, measure each side to be sure your piece will not be skewed.

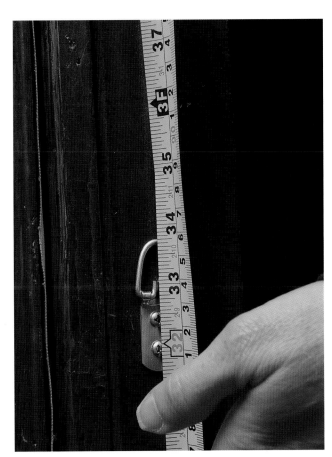

7. Add the two measurements together to get the distance your hangers need to be from the top of the sofa. (33⅝ + 10 = 43⅝ inches)

8. From the center point of the back of the sofa, measure up this distance . . .

. . . and mark the point. This is your horizontal center point.

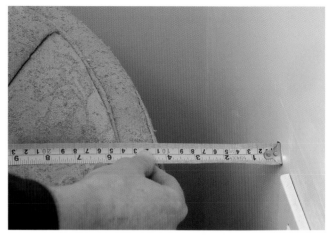

9. To get your vertical center point, first measure from one edge of the couch to the nearest wall, and *add* that to the center measurement of the sofa. Here, that distance is 4 inches, so we add that to our center point measurement and get 32½ inches.

10. In the approximate area of your horizontal center point, measure out from the corner along the wall 32½ inches and make another pencil mark.

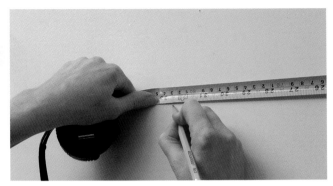

The mark represents the vertical center point of your framing project.

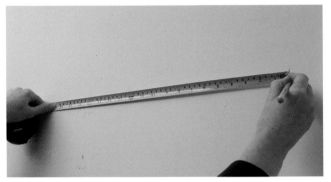

11. You now need to measure out 17 inches (half the distance between the hangers) on each side of the center point. Make a small pencil mark at 17 inches on each side of your vertical center point.

12. Place the level with the bottom edge touching the vertical center point (the mark you made by measuring out from the wall).

13. Find the marks you made at 17 inches, and draw a small horizontal line with your pencil against the level, even with the marks.

The marks should be close enough to the level that you can easily see where to draw the line. If the distance is very great, you should recheck your measurements and try again.

14. Place the level vertically along the first pencil marks you made at 17 inches. Align the level so it is straight . . .

95

. . . and inscribe another small line across each of the horizontal lines you just drew.

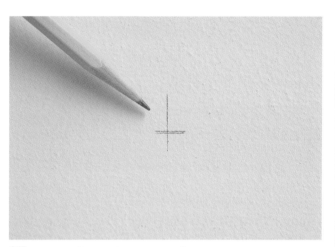

15. You will now have a small cross marked on the wall, with the intersection at the precise spot you need to place your hanger.

Single Hangers

If placing one single hanger, you need only to mark the center spot where the wire or the saw-tooth hanger will be affixed. To do this, follow the same steps as above for finding the center point, and then use the level to find the precise point at which to place the hanger.

Picture Hangers

1. When using a hanger with a nail at the top and the hook below, remember *not* to drive the nail precisely into the center of your cross. The cross is where the hanger must be, not the nail.

Tap the nail into place with a hammer. You may wish to drill a small hole first, in order not to damage the wall any more than necessary. Use a bit small enough to leave you some resistance putting in the nail; otherwise, the hole may be too big to hold the nail and the hanger will not support the frame.

A correctly placed hanger.

2. Once you have your hangers set, move the picture into place in front of the hangers.

3. Holding it slightly out from the wall, slide your fingers around behind the edge of the frame . . .

. . . and loop the frame over the hangers, one side at a time.

97

4. Gently lower the bottom of the frame against the wall, making sure your bump-ons meet the wall first. If they don't, you can move them to the proper position and press them into place again.

Molly Bolts

Molly bolts are simply long bolts with a special sleeve around them that can be driven into the wall for extra support. The sleeve holds the bolt and the frame tight to the wall, while the bolt itself is unscrewed partway to allow the hanger to be put over it. The advantages of molly bolts are that they are durable and will support heavy frames and mirrors; the disadvantages are that they are difficult to remove from walls and will leave a much bigger mark than a simple nail-in hanger. If you are concerned about damaging a wall, if you think you will be moving the piece frequently, or if the piece you are hanging is not particularly heavy, choose the standard hangers instead.

1. To use molly bolts, you will need a drill to make a hole in the wall at the center point of your pencilled cross. Use a bit big enough to allow you to get the bolt into the wall, but not so big that the bolt is loose.

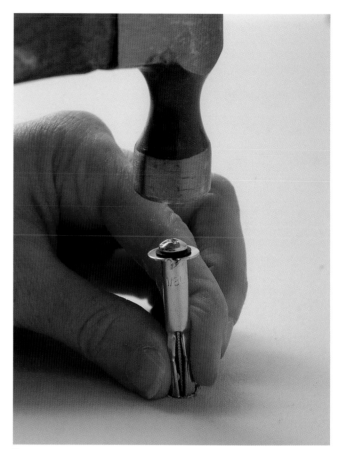

2. With a hammer, tap the molly bolt all the way into the wall.

Do not angle the bolt at all, but drive it straight in. It will still provide enough support for a heavy frame.

3. With a screwdriver or drill, tighten the screw so that it is nearly flush with the end of the sleeve. This helps set it into the wall. Don't screw it in *too* tightly, or it will be hard to get out again, but make sure the sleeve of the bolt is firmly and fully in the wall.

4. Then unscrew the bolt ⅛ to ¼ inch.

The sleeve will remain embedded in the wall, and you will have room to place the loop of the mirror hanger or wire over the edge of the screw onto the bolt behind it.

5. Place the hangers over the set molly bolts and you are done.

Resources

BOOKS

Bartholomew, Lee. *Picture Framing for the First Time.* New York: Sterling Publishing Co., Inc., 2004.

Oberrecht, Kenn. *Home Book of Picture Framing, Second Edition: Professional Secrets of Mounting, Matting, Framing, and Displaying Artwork, Photographs, Posters, Fabrics, Collectibles, Carvings, and More.* Mechanicsburg, PA: Stackpole Books, 1998.

Stokes, Penelope. *Picture Framing Made Easy.* London: Cassell & Company, 1996.

Thompson, Janean. *Matting and Framing Made Easy: Step-by-Step Easy-to-Master Techniques for the Beginning Framer.* New York: Watson-Guptill Publications, 1996.

EQUIPMENT AND SUPPLIES

Craft and Art Supply Stores

Many craft stores carry some matting supplies and a selection of ready-made frames. Art supply stores are more likely to have the things you need for matting and mounting. Check your local telephone directory for a listing of craft stores in your area.

A.C. Moore
www.acmoore.com

Ben Franklin
www.benfranklinstores.com

Dick Blick Art Materials
(800) 828-4548
www.dickblick.com

Hobby Lobby
(800) 888-0321
www.hobbylobby.com

Michael's
(800) 642-4235
www.michaels.com

Building Supply Retailers

Check your local telephone directory for lumberyards and building supply retailers, which often carry molding and other materials suitable for building frames.

The Home Depot
(800) 553-3199
www.homedepot.com

Lowe's Home Improvement
(800) 445-6937
www.lowes.com

Online Suppliers and Resources

American Frame Corporation
888-628-3833
www.americanframe.com

Framing 4 Yourself
(800) 246-4726
www.framing4yourself.com

FramingSupplies.com
(800) 334-9060
www.framingsupplies.com

PictureFrames.com
(800) 221-0262
www.pictureframes.com

Picture Framing Magazine Online
www.pictureframingmagazine.com
Features many useful links to suppliers

Stackpole Basics

All the Skills and Tools You Need to Get Started

- **Straightforward, expert instruction on a variety of crafts, hobbies, and sports**
- **Step-by-step, easy-to-follow format**
- **Current information on equipment and prices for the beginner**
- **Full-color photography and illustrations**
- **Convenient lay-flat spiral binding**

BASIC KNITTING
$19.95, 128 pages, 377 photos, 50 illustrations, 0-8117-3109-X

BASIC CANDLE MAKING
$19.95, 104 pages, 600 photos, 0-8117-2476-X

BASIC STAINED GLASS MAKING
$19.95, 144 pages, 754 color photos, 24 illustrations, 0-8117-2846-3

BASIC WOODWORKING
$19.95, 80 pages, 303 color photos, 0-8117-3113-8

BASIC DRIED FLOWER ARRANGING
$16.95, 96 pages, 234 color photos, 0-8117-2863-3

Available at your favorite craft shop or bookstore, or from Stackpole Books at (800) 732-3669

STACKPOLE BOOKS

www.stackpolebooks.com